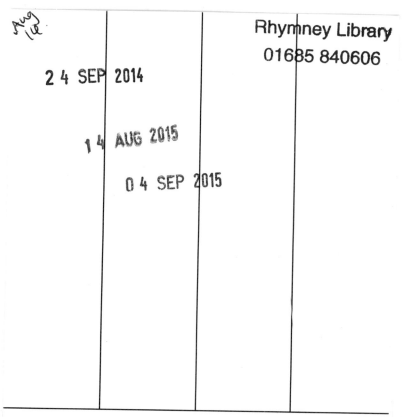

CCBC
AMAZON
8/2014

This is a true story. Some of the names of places, groups, people, and my deceased friend and his family, have been changed for privacy reasons.

ISBN 13: 9781493643721
ISBN: 149364372X

DEDICATION

To my friend Paul who kept his promise;
And to my parents, who have both crossed over now.
My everlasting gratitude for your love, support and believing in me
always.
May you all have eternal joy and peace.

ACKNOWLEDGEMENTS

When I first entertained the idea of writing a book, urged by friends and family members after hearing about the unusual and strange events that happened at my deceased friend's estate, I had no idea where this journey would take me. ESTATE OF HORROR's structure did not rely solely on the detailed diary entries I kept or our personal experiences; the chapters dealt with eyewitness accounts, various people who encountered the poltergeist activity for themselves, EVP recordings, audio and visual evidence and secret documents discovered that had a profound effect on the overall mystery of why the house became haunted.

My experiences with writing my book have been collaborative, and I attribute the successful completion of my book to not only myself but to everyone who helped and encouraged me along the way; and the generosity of family members and friends who gave me permission to use their photos, experiences and testimonies included in the book.

Of those people I would like to thank, foremost is my literary agent Laurie Hawkins, who has become a good friend and whose great advice, faith in my abilities and belief in my terrifying story never wavered. It was a brave act for her to sign me to a contract, as she has been the recipient of some strange paranormal activity since taking me on as a client.

Very special thanks go to my son, Chris. Without his hard work helping me at the house, his love and support – and sense of humor during the really scary times – I could never have done any of this or perhaps even survive. I feel truly blessed!

TABLE OF CONTENTS

FOREWORD

I am a psychic medium and paranormal investigator. In the twenty-plus years that I have been investigating, I have been called to many unusual cases and have traveled the world to investigate the paranormal. In 2009, I was contacted by Anita Jo Intenzo to help her with some paranormal issues she was experiencing at the home of a friend whose estate she had been placed in charge of. The desperation in her voice when I spoke to her prompted me to visit as soon as I possibly could. I never dreamed that this phone call was the start of a journey that would lead me to be faced with new and even terrifying possibilities in the world of the supernatural.

On the surface, it seemed like an intelligent haunting; shadowy figures were seen and small objects were being thrown. It sounded like someone just wanted attention. I had no idea that in taking this case I was entering into one of the most unusual and compelling cases of my career.

ESTATE OF HORROR is a true story. This story offers proof that the supernatural does exist, right alongside us, and can enter our lives when we least expect it in ways that are enlightening, frightening, disturbing and violent. As shocking, unnerving and unbelievable as ESTATE OF HORROR may be, Anita Jo Intenzo lived with it and I experienced it.

Come with us now as we journey through the experiences that tested our faith and even our sanity. Welcome to the *Estate of Horror*.

Laurie Hull
November, 2013

INTRODUCTION

When we told my parents what had happened, they were afraid for our safety. "You're not going back there, are you?" they asked.

Now you would think that after our terrifying paranormal experiences, my son and I would choose to never set foot in Paul's house again. No one would have blamed us for doing so. I have no doubt that many people in our situation would have been scared, but we were not afraid at that point.

Chris and I had always been fans of science fiction and loved monster movies so we didn't scare easily. Perhaps we were naïve because we had never encountered anything like this and there wasn't a point of reference.

We didn't believe we were in any danger.

We were wrong.

I.

A SUDDEN LOSS

"Each departed friend is a magnet that attracts us to the next world."
- Jean Paul Richter

Chapter 1

THE PHONE CALL

People say that a single moment can change a life. My moment was Monday morning January 19, 2009, when I received a phone call that forever altered my life and introduced me to things I never thought could be possible.

I had intended to call my good friend Paul when I finished breakfast. We had known each other for thirty years. I couldn't stop thinking about him over the weekend and felt it was important to reach out to schedule time for lunch at my house. We hadn't seen each other at Christmas when we usually exchanged gifts because my close friend, Rose, had lost her mother to a sudden heart attack a week before the holiday. Rose was like a sister to me and I wanted to do whatever I could to support her during the tough time of having to bury her mother the day before Christmas Eve.

I had just entered my art studio when the phone rang; the clock read 9:35 A.M. I picked up the receiver thinking it was probably my mother and hoping it was nothing serious. I loved my parents, but I was dreading it could be more bad news.

I didn't recognize the voice on the other end of the phone.

"Hello, is this Anita Intenzo?"

"Yes?"

"Do you know Paul Jaeger?"

"Yes, he's a dear friend of mine. What's wrong?"

"This is Dr. Hammond at Springfield Hospital. "Your friend is here and he's gravely ill."

I barely knew what to say. "What happened? Does he have pneumonia?"

All I could think of was that he had an ongoing asthma problem for years, and perhaps it had gotten worse with a cold. The last time he came over for "Dunch" (his play on words—too late for lunch, but too early for dinner) he appeared to be in fine physical shape. But he had used his inhaler several times during the meal and told me that his asthma had been bad lately.

"No, he's had a massive heart attack," the doctor said.

No words came. *He's never complained about his heart or anything related to that, what could have happened?* He had a trainer and worked out regularly, ate healthily and always watched the fat content in his food.

My thoughts returned to reality when I heard the doctor's voice. "Your name was in his wallet to call in case of emergency. We are letting you know that he's in the process of being moved to Crozer Chester Hospital, to their Cardiac Wing for further care."

"Wait. Can't I see him?" I asked frantically. "I'll come over right now to be with him. I want to go with him."

The doctor interrupted. "That's not possible. He's on a ventilator and he isn't conscious, and is being moved right away. We'll call you when he gets to Crozer Chester Hospital and keep you posted. Does he have any other family?"

"He has a brother, but I don't know his number. I have to call his lawyer and ask him if he has it," I said.

I thanked the doctor and hung up the phone, overwhelmed by what he had told me. My emotions were jumbled and I didn't know what to do first.

My son Chris, 25, was just coming down the stairs, ready to grab a quick breakfast and head to work.

"What's going on, Mom?" he asked.

I started to cry. "Paul's had a heart attack."

I looked at my son's face and saw my news surprised him. "What do you have to do?" he asked.

"I have to find that envelope that he gave me with his lawyer's name on it."

I immediately opened the top drawer of my desk to look for the envelope and thankful that Paul had given me the emergency numbers in April 2008 before he left for Europe. When I got them, I wrote *Paul's Important Papers* on the envelope in red ink and put it in my desk's top drawer.

I dialed the lawyer's number and told him the news.

"How bad is it, Anita?" he asked.

"It's bad, Jeff. Of course they won't commit to his chances of survival. I'll have to wait for the hospital to call me with an update, but it doesn't look good."

"I'm shocked, he's a young guy," the lawyer said.

"I know. He's only 55."

"Call me and keep me updated, Anita."

"I will, Jeff. Thank you." I hung up the phone and just sat for a moment trying to digest everything that had just happened.

The next few hours were a blur. First, I called my mother. I tried to soften the blow as best I could, but I know my mother saw right through me. She was fond of Paul and over the years had invited him over for home-cooked Italian meals. The news shocked her, too.

"How... terrible," she said. "What are you going to do?"

I started to cry again. "I don't know, Mom. I'll take it one step at a time."

"If there's anything I can do..." My mother's voice trailed off because we both knew there wasn't.

"I will call you when I know more about his condition," and hung up the phone.

Next, I got in touch with Ray Connors, who ran a pet service and took care of Paul's beloved cats, Cleo and Alexia, when Paul was away, and his friend Jane Castor, both of whom were surprised and saddened with the news.

Dr. Shankar, the cardiologist, finally called from Crozer at 1:00 PM and told me they were taking Paul to the operating room but his chances for survival were not good.

"He has about a 5-10% chance. We're doing everything we can do to save him," the doctor said.

Again, I was so stunned I didn't know what to say. I called the lawyer and told him I was leaving for the hospital immediately. As I drove there, my mind kept going back to the last time Paul and I were together. We had talked for several hours about our favorite subject - history - and he told me he wanted to get started on an expanded article he'd written several years earlier about my work with antique dolls. A local newspaper had published the article and it was well received. I had gotten some nice business from the publicity.

"I hope the revised article helps your business even more," Paul had said to me with a smile on his face.

"It was such a big help the last time, I can't ask for any more Paul."

Paul winked at me. "Yes, you can. You deserve it."

His generosity was one of the many reasons why I loved him. When he left that day, I gave him an extra hug and told him to take care of himself.

He kissed me on the cheek. "Ok, I'll see you soon."

If I'd only known that was the last time I'd see him alive.

—⁓—

It was snowing and a bitter wind was blowing when I arrived at the hospital. The uncertainty and grief I felt made the cold wind bite even colder. I walked across the parking lot, praying with each step and hoping that the news would be good, but fearing in my heart that it wouldn't be. I didn't know where to go and it took me several minutes to find someone who could tell me what happened to Paul.

I sat for over an hour in the waiting room before someone came in and asked me to follow them to the Catheterization Lab. I knew all about "Cath Labs" because my mother had two catheterizations and stents placed in both the right and left arteries to her heart to unblock them. It saved her life and I prayed that Paul's catheterization might let him live too. That false hope was shattered when I was led down the hall and came face to face with a group of grim-faced doctors. As soon as I saw them, I knew that Paul was dead.

I learned that he had called 911 the previous night when he couldn't catch his breath and been taken to the hospital. I was upset to hear that he'd waited outside in the snow, sitting on a bench, with the house locked up tight. He probably thought he was having an asthma attack and would have an overnight stay in the hospital, not realizing he would never return home.

When they finally had him on the operating table, his blood pressure crashed and they couldn't attempt to operate. There would have been no point to it. He was gone. Later, I learned that they discovered he'd had a heart attack several days earlier because they could see dead muscle and tissue on their scans. A blocked artery caused severe pressure and finally ruptured the wall on one side of his heart. There was a large hole there now that couldn't be repaired.

The doctors were apologetic. "We're sorry, it was too late to operate," they said. "The damage to his heart was too extensive."

"We are sorry for your loss," they offered. "But you should know that he didn't suffer."

"So, he literally died of a broken heart," I said with tears in my eyes.

"You could say that," one doctor said. "Again, I'm very sorry."

I couldn't hear anything else; tears filled my eyes and were soon streaming down my cheeks. I was lead to a small room where I could say goodbye.

The scene was surreal. He lay there with a sheet pulled up to his chest and the ventilator tube still off to one side of his mouth. He'd died all alone with no one there, not even me, to comfort him.

"Paul, I'm here sweetheart. They wouldn't let me see you until now. I'm so sorry. Oh, Paul, why didn't you call someone sooner? What's the big idea you leaving me behind like this? We were going to write a book together. We had plans."

Did I think he'd respond to my admonishment? The small room was still and silent except for the annoying humming noise from the harsh overhead florescent lights. I stared at him, not wanting to believe he was gone. I thought I'd be afraid being left alone in the room with a dead body but I wasn't. That surprised me. How could I be afraid of him; this was my good friend with whom I'd spent so many happy times.

I burst into tears again. I spent several more minutes with him, stroking his hair, and then I kissed him on the forehead, feeling that he was already cold. Out of my numbed shock, I suddenly felt a sense of duty and role of protector. Paul needed me now more than ever. I held his hand one last time.

"Don't worry, Paul, I'll take care of everything."

Chapter 2
BONDS OF FRIENDSHIP

The holidays had been difficult. In attending the funeral for Rose's mother, it was certainly capping off a very traumatic year for me. The health of my parents had also been failing for some time. 2008 had been a horrendous year for my mother, who at 85, was in and out of the hospital with one health crisis after another. She had suffered a heart attack at the end of April and I spent much of May and June making 911 calls as she suffered one setback after another. When she wasn't in the hospital, I was shuttling her back and forth for tests and doctor's visits.

While my mother was in the hospital, my son and I took care of my 86-year-old father, who suffered from Parkinson's disease. We helped him with his meals, made sure he was taking his medication, and paid the bills. We were lucky that I was a freelance artist. I had a flexible schedule and my son's hours had been cut from work recently, so we were able to be there for Mom and Dad as much as they needed. My brother and his wife did what they could, but it was difficult for them to be on call 24/7 the way my son and I were. My sister-in-law and her mother cooked meals and sent them over, which we appreciated.

In between all this, I was trying to find the time to work on my clients' projects, sometimes working until midnight because I never knew what the next day would bring or when my mother would call needing help. After suffering for several hours, she would finally call and the argument would begin.

"Do you think I'm sick enough to call 911?" she would ask.

"Only you know how bad you feel, Mom," I would say. "But to be on the safe side I think you should."

Sometimes she would and sometimes she wouldn't. This went on for months. I adored my parents, especially my father, and was trying to be a "good Italian daughter." They relied on me for almost everything and hadn't accepted the fact that they had gotten older and needed help.

In the fall, my mother seemed to improve until in the middle of the night she fell in the bathroom and broke her right wrist. By January 2009 when Paul died, she'd been in and out of the hospital nine times.

—⁂—

I met Paul at a community library when we both attended a lecture on the early Native American Indian tribes. The small crowd was attentive and the professor who spoke gave a very interesting talk about the research he'd done on the subject. When the lecture was over, I saw Paul walking towards me with a big smile on his face.

"I'm glad you asked that question because I was thinking of asking him the same thing. It was very smart of you." He extended his hand. "I'm Paul Jaeger."

"Anita Intenzo," I replied and shook his hand.

We began to talk about history and archaeology, two subjects we both adored. The conversation continued out into the parking lot and I couldn't help thinking that I had never met anyone like him. He had an old world style and mannerisms with a certain European sophistication. He stood ramrod straight, was highly intelligent and very nice. He seemed to be a unique individual worth getting to know. In this way, our friendship of thirty years began.

I was more than a little intrigued by him and over time, our friendship grew. We would spend hours talking about interests we shared: history, ancient Egypt, Greece, and Rome, Native American Indians, books, the arts, cultural events, the West and many other things. Paul was very cultured and loved old and new movies, Broadway shows, and all kinds of music, especially German composers. He was fiercely proud of his German-American heritage and spoke fluent German.

He was a big fan of Julie Andrews and the movie *The Sound of Music*. Years earlier, Paul had visited the von Trapp family ski lodge in Stowe, Vermont and had gotten to know the Baroness Maria von Trapp quite well. They even corresponded for many years.

He was an avid reader and considered books old friends. He was a writer and sent volumes of letters to celebrities and heads of state throughout the world. He composed beautiful letters to family and friends. He would have nothing to do with computers or e-mail.

"I'll be the last holdout for the dying written word," he once told me.

I was proud of all the wonderful cards and letters he sent me through the years and admired his beautiful handwriting and the effort he put into writing a well-thought-out letter. I never saw a mistake in his letters, as they were always written perfectly. Later, I learned his secret. I discovered drafts of pre-letters written on scraps of paper among his things, which solved the mystery of why I never found any mistakes. I realized I would miss getting his cards and letters.

Paul wrote numerous articles for local newspapers that, along with various part-time jobs, provided him with enough of an income to travel and research future articles. The breadth of his knowledge was astounding, everything from Monarch butterflies to the European Monarchy, one of his passions.

Now that passion was silent.

—◌—

I left the hospital with a brown bag that contained the last items of clothing that Paul wore, including some keys in his pants pocket. When I got home, I called the lawyer, who was very sad to hear my news about Paul.

"Anita, do you want me to call his brother? I know there was bad blood between them," he said.

I remember Paul once telling me that if anything happened to him not to tell his brother. "You know Jeff, I think that's the right thing to do. I don't care what happened between him and his brother in the past. Please call him and give him the bad news." I started tearing up again.

"I agree with you, Anita. I'll make the call."

I thanked him and dialed Ray Connors to ask if he could meet me at the house that night with the set of keys Paul had given him in April. I was hoping they matched mine and that we would find out what door they opened. Ray was not allowed in the house without my presence, for no one, except me, as his executrix under Pennsylvania law, had the right to enter the property of the deceased person.

It was dark by the time Chris and I pulled up to Paul's ranch style home. I had never met Ray before and I was glad I had my son there for much needed moral support. Ray was waiting for us in his truck.

"I'm so sorry about Paul. He was a good guy," Ray said as he shook my hand. "I imagine you knew him for some time."

"Yes," I said. "About thirty years."

Ray nodded and looked at me sympathetically. He showed me his key and it matched one I found in a side pocket of Paul's pants. We tried to open the side door to the enclosed porch but the key wouldn't turn. After a few minutes we were convinced we would have to call a locksmith. Ray decided to try it again and this time he was able to open the lock by turning the key a certain way. Then I tried my key again and with his instructions, I was able to open the door on my own. From that day on, I was the only one who had the knack of opening that door. We then used the other key to open the kitchen door and the alarm went off. It made a loud, penetrating noise that reverberated throughout the house.

"Do you know what the code is, Ray?" I asked him, starting to panic.

"No, I don't. Paul didn't have the security system armed when I took care of his cats last April."

We fully expected the police to show up at any moment, but the initial alarm stopped after a few minutes and they didn't. The alarm went on motion detection mode and we figured that since the police didn't show up he was using the loud alarm to deter intruders. I was grateful that I didn't have to explain anything to the police because I was exhausted emotionally. Later that week, the security company reinstated the alarm and rebooted it with a new code so I could sleep at night, knowing the house was secure when I wasn't there.

It was so eerie to be in Paul's house. I felt like an intruder barging into someone's home in the middle of his everyday routine. What I would find would be astounding.

As we walked through the dimly lit kitchen, the huge piles of papers and other things on the counters, the kitchen table, the chairs and the floor shocked me. We had to walk single file because there was no more room. I couldn't believe my eyes. The kitchen was a dirty mess; the sink filled with unwashed dishes and glasses, and a spoon stuck in a pot with food debris all over the stove. The place smelled of trapped cooking odors, dust and mothballs. I hadn't been invited to his house for over two years and couldn't believe Paul had been living this way. I couldn't recall the house ever smelling like this when I'd visit him. When his parents were alive, the house was always tidy, warm and inviting and his mother especially made me feel welcome.

We walked through the dining room and living room where we turned a light on and saw more piles of paper, junk mail, newspapers, bags, gift-wrap and Christmas gifts covering the sofa and chairs. Debris covered the floors, too. I was embarrassed for Paul. Ray had no reaction to this and walked to another room to check on the cats.

"They're fine," he said and went to clean the litter box, then walked into the kitchen and filled the cats' bowls with food.

Every time someone moved, the motion detector in the living room beeped. "That's really annoying," Chris said. "Can't you shut it off?"

"Not without Paul's password and I'm not sure his lawyer has it."

We looked at each shaking our heads. "How could he let it get this bad?" I asked. "I don't understand how he could live this way."

"I don't know, Mom. He must have been really sick for a while," Chris said.

I looked down at the floor and its rust orange carpet, straight out of the eighties and noticed that near the table lamp was a small area free of debris that was just the right size for someone to sit. Paul's typewriter and research papers were strewn around the empty spot. Not far from that was a round stool with a small portable TV on it, which he must have watched while he worked. Near the wall stood a faux marble statue on a pedestal of the "Veiled Lady" by the sculptor Raphaelle Monti. I had seen Paul pull this piece from storage and use this replica in several of his Victorian history lectures but hadn't realized he keep it out all the time. She depicted a bride from the 1850's caught in a serene pose before her wedding but she now reminded me, given the sad circumstances of my friend's sudden death, of a woman veiled in mourning.

Looking around the room and despite all the junk everywhere, the house seemed so empty and silent. I shook my head in amazement and thought, *how could he live like this?* I felt so bad for him. We pushed some papers on the floor aside and put a timer on one of the lamps.

Ray came back into the room and I turned to him. "I'm in a bind, Ray. I don't have a cat and I don't know how to take care of them. Since they know you, would you mind coming over here every day to feed them and take care of them? I trust you."

"Sure, I could do that," Ray said.

At least that solved one problem temporarily, but if I had any idea at that moment what lay ahead of me, I would have walked out the door and never come back.

Chapter 3

THE EXECUTRIX

The next morning, I arrived at the lawyer's office. We had to go to the County Courthouse across the street from his office to probate the will and I figured it was best if I got there early. I was nervous meeting him. The lawyer's office appeared disorganized with stacks of files about the room and the papers piled on his desk reminded me of Paul's place. *Oh, brother,* I thought, *didn't I just leave something like this at Paul's house?* However, Jeff seemed affable.

I sat down near his desk, being careful not to disturb a pile of papers that were sitting precariously by the edge. He slid a copy of the will he had drawn up for Paul in 2002 towards me and asked me to read it.

"Anita, you are the sole executrix of the estate and have power of attorney," Jeff said.

I was more than a bit shocked when he told me what that entailed. I was the only one who would be able to sign checks, and according to the lawyer, had been given the "keys to the kingdom." I looked through what turned out to be a seven page, detailed will while I tried to understand the legal terms the lawyer was using.

Probate means to validate a will. We had to state for the record that Paul was officially dead and that his death certificate was registered by the court. We also had to establish the fact that I had the "Power of Attorney." Jeff continued to rattle off a list of things to be done next and I tried to take it all in. I had never been an executor of anyone's estate, and it was all new to me. I was facing a huge responsibility.

"I called Carl last night and he was really devastated over his brother's death," Jeff said.

I looked up at him. "I'm glad you did. He should know what happened to his brother, no matter what kind of relationship they had. It's over now that Paul is dead."

"I agree with you, Anita. You have a big job ahead of you and a ton of phone calls to make. I need you to look for all financial records. You also need to look for records of all bills, tax and bank statements and anything else that pertains to the estate."

I nodded as I took it all in.

The lawyer continued. "I have a deposition in court this morning and I have to leave soon. Why don't you go over to Springfield and pick up Paul's other personal effects. I'll be on vacation next week, but I'll see you before I leave," he added.

Our meeting was over and I left his office, thinking that I had my work cut out for me but hardly knew where to begin. I wasn't going to get any help from Paul's family and knew I was on my own. I felt numb. People think that being the executor of an estate is glamorous. I have news for them; it isn't. It is a lot of hard work with little thanks. Yes, you receive a fee for your services, depending on the amount the estate is worth; in Pennsylvania, it is 5% of the total value of the estate. However, there is a catch: if an estate is worth up to $300,000-$500,000, the percentage goes down. My dear friend had asked me to be executor in 2007 and I had accepted. What else could I have done? He had assured me that if I accepted he would "take care" of me. I also knew Paul didn't trust anyone as much as he did me to carry out his final wishes. Besides, he didn't have anyone else since he was estranged from his brother.

I really didn't know how much he was concerned about me until our last "Dunch" when he told me about an annuity he had set up for me. He had lost several thousand dollars in it with the volatile financial market, but he was thankful it hadn't been worse. He mentioned the amount and the name of the annuity, which I had never heard of and had no knowledge of without seeing his will. I was flabbergasted that he would do such a thing for me. I told him so, but he just shrugged it off.

I think he may have had a premonition about not living to a ripe old age, but he joked about it. I couldn't bear the thought that he was serious. Later, I learned that the amount of the annuity in the will was actually one-third the amount Paul had told me. I was disappointed. The financial agent and the attorney had no answers for me, except that Paul either lied to me or was mixed up about what annuity he left me.

I had months of backbreaking labor ahead of me before we settled the estate. I was hurt that my friend had possibly deceived me about the true amount of the annuity and the deplorable conditions at his house. I now felt he had taken advantage of our friendship. Did he think I might not agree to be his executor if he hadn't offered the annuity and mention its worth? In all honesty, he was trying to repaint and fix up his living room the past several months. It's just that no one would have imagined him dying so suddenly and so young. So was there blame to go around? *The keys to the kingdom,* the lawyer had said. I thought of it more like the keys to a nightmare, and that is exactly what it became. If I had known then, what I know now, I would never have consented to being his executor.

Then there would be no story.

—⁂—

I left the lawyer's office and went to the hospital to retrieve Paul's personal effects. I had a copy of the death certificate and the "Short," a legal document that stated that I had power of attorney and was the executor of the estate. I signed for his effects and they handed me a bag with his wallet, keys, glasses, inhaler, pen and writing pad. I barely glanced at them and headed for his house to check on things.

I was starting to see this as a bad joke and imagined myself just going over to see if Paul was home. I pulled into the driveway and saw in the daylight how overgrown the bushes were that led up to the side porch door. The previous night I had been so upset I hadn't noticed how foreboding the place looked. The key was a problem again, but I finally got the door open and went inside. The smell in the kitchen was atrocious. In the daylight, everything looked worse than it had the night before. I stacked the papers in the living room off to the side, so Ray wouldn't step on any important ones when he came there to take care of the cats.

I was only in the house for about an hour when someone knocked on the side porch door. I opened the door and Paul's brother, Carl, walked in. I looked at him with tears in my eyes and he looked at me with a mixture of sadness, anger and mistrust.

"Oh, Carl, I'm so sorry about your brother," I said.

He just stood in the kitchen and looked at me. "What's going on? What happened?" he asked.

If looks could kill, you'd be six feet under, I thought.

"What did the lawyer tell you?" I asked.

"I was on my way to his office for an appointment and decided to come by the house. I saw a car in the driveway so I thought I'd better check things out," he said.

My guard immediately went up because I knew he didn't have an appointment with the lawyer since Jeff told me he was running late for a deposition at the courthouse. He wasn't telling the truth. Carl lived over an hour away and decided to make the long trek without a scheduled appointment? Yeah, right. What was he up to? I was going to be very careful of what I said.

"Look Carl, I was just at the lawyer's office and he's on his way to court. He won't be in his office. I'm glad you stopped here, though."

I knew that Carl hadn't been allowed in the house when Paul was alive, but I let him inside. I wasn't sure if the lawyer would be happy about what I was doing, but felt it was the right thing to do. He started to roam around the house with me following close behind. I was very uncomfortable the whole time because I hadn't seen Carl since his mother's funeral and memorial in 2001. I'd never had an argument with him, but I knew he and Paul had a strained relationship for the last eight years. I had taken Paul's side because I believed my friend had suffered insults, accusations and slights through the years and felt Carl and his wife Doris' treatment of him justified his attitude.

Carl continued to look around and started to shake his head. I knew what he was thinking: *this place never looked like this while his mother was alive.* It was embarrassing. I did my best to be friendly. "I just contacted the funeral director and maybe we should go over the things we need to do next," I said.

"Whatever you want to do," Carl said. "Do you mind if my wife comes in?"

Paul had despised his sister-in-law.

"Do you mean that your wife has been sitting in the car all this time?" I asked. "Of course, let her come in."

She came in the door. "Doris, do you remember Anita?" Carl asked.

She looked at me harshly. "No, I don't remember you."

Paul would be yelling at me right now for letting them both in, I thought. I glared at her. "But I remember *you,*" I said.

I didn't say any more, knowing full well that she had seen me numerous times with Paul at family events and was perhaps baiting me for an argument. I was not falling for it. This wasn't the time for a family squabble. I tried to clear off the sofa and chairs so we could wait for the funeral director to arrive. I had called him per Paul's instructions in the will. Doris sat down on one of the chairs and Carl sat on the sofa; both looked around disapprovingly.

"How long is this going to take?" she asked impatiently.

"I called Mr. Knox and he said he'd be here in about twenty minutes."

I knew that the less I said the better off I would be. After all, they were in the house because I had allowed them to be there; under the law, I didn't have to let them in. They kept whispering and shaking their heads over the condition of the house.

The phone rang. It was Paul's personal trainer calling from the gym. He wanted to know why Paul had missed his appointment since it was so unlike him. He was completely shocked when I gave him the bad news.

"I can't believe it!" he said. "Why didn't he tell me he had heart problems? He must have known."

"I don't know," I said.

"It's so unbelievable because he was in the best shape of his life. If there's anything I can do, please let me know."

I received another phone call several minutes later.

"Where's Paul?"

It was the little elderly woman that Paul took shopping every Tuesday. I remembered him mentioning her several times.

"He was supposed to take me grocery shopping this morning," she said. "Where is he?"

My voice cracked as I told Peggy the bad news.

"Who's that?" Carl asked angrily.

I quickly got off the phone and explained whom Peggy was and what a shock it was for her to learn of Paul's death.

Carl was becoming increasingly more agitated.

"Please take it easy," I said.

"Why don't I have a copy of Paul's will?' Carl asked me abruptly and looked at his wife.

I took out my copy and showed it to him. "It's all there, Carl. I'm the executor and I'm going to do my best to follow Paul's wishes," I said. "If you want a copy I'll call the lawyer and tell him to give you one."

He seemed satisfied for the moment and I was glad to see the funeral director, Mr. Knox, at the kitchen door. He knew the Jaeger family well as he had been the undertaker for both Mr. and Mrs. Jaeger. We went over a list of things to be done and he had us sign forms so he could have Paul's body released from the hospital morgue. The funeral director collected some family information for the obituary and we chose a design for his prayer cards. I would have to call the pastor of the local church Paul had selected for his memorial service and arrange with her, too. Mr. Knox then showed us a catalogue and asked us to pick out a memorial container for Paul's cremated ashes.

"Why is he being cremated?" Carl asked. He seemed stunned at this revelation.

"That's what he wanted," I said.

"Can't we bury his ashes in my parents' burial plot?"

"No," I said. "He wanted his ashes to be taken out west and scattered on a mountain top."

Carl became very upset. "What was wrong with him? Even in death he wants to be as far away from us as possible."

That started a long list of questions concerning what was wrong with Paul; that he must have been both mentally and physically sick. Why didn't he get help sooner? Why didn't he let his family in the house for the past eight years? Why did he keep to himself and never show up for family events? It was a tidal wave of anger and raw emotion. Carl's wife did her best to put her two cents in.

I had no answers for them and decided to keep my opinions to myself.

"You only heard Paul's side of the story," Carl said. "You don't know what we went through."

The conversation seemed to embarrass the funeral director and I was thankful when he stopped the one-sided argument.

"Please, we need to stay on task and get these things taken care of," he said.

"Yes," I said firmly. "Can we please concentrate on getting Paul out of the morgue so Mr. Knox can take care of him?"

That statement ended the bickering for the moment. We finished with the details, with me making most of the decisions. I tried to defer to Carl's preferences, but he had little to say. We finally pinned him down for a time the following week that he would be able to make the memorial service, which prompted his wife to say, "I won't be coming."

When everything looked to be in order, Carl and his wife got up to leave. The funeral director had gone out to his car to get some sample prayer cards for me to look at and I was alone with Carl and Doris in the kitchen.

"I have a real problem with a stranger looking through all my family's private papers," Carl said. "I don't think it's right."

I tried to stay calm, but I was boiling mad. "Look, Carl, I'm sorry it turned out this way, I truly am, but Paul put me in charge and I have to respect and carry out his last wishes to the best of my ability. The last thing I want to do is get in the middle of a family feud. He's gone and whatever went on between you should end with his death."

I had their undivided attention so I paused for the moment.

"I'm not a stranger. Paul and I knew each other for thirty years. I knew your mother and father too. Paul considered my son and me as close to a family he'd ever have." I made that extra point directed squarely to his wife.

Without saying a word, they turned and left and I let out a sigh of relief.

Chapter 4

THE MEMORIAL

I was solely responsible for arranging Paul's memorial service, which I scheduled for January 29. The days following his death were a blur of activity. I made all the plans without interference from his family or his lawyer and decided to trust my instincts on what Paul would have wanted me to do. He'd specified certain things in his will and I built on that. We shared a long history together as friends and I kept thinking *what would Paul like?* One thing the lawyer told me immediately was that Paul stated in his will that after his cremation he wanted me to spread his ashes on top of a mountain in the southwest. After a long conversation with the lawyer, I told him I could not do it at this time because there was too much going on. Jeff suggested that since he was going to Vail, Colorado the following week to go skiing, would it be all right for him to spread Paul's ashes on a mountaintop in Vail.

"Is Colorado considered part of the southwest?" Jeff asked.

"Yes," I said. "That will work."

Since special paperwork was necessary to carry human remains on a plane, it was better that an attorney handled that legality for me, too.

I went to the house several times during that first week to look for the papers Jeff would need to contact the financial institutions that handled the funds for the beneficiaries in the will. There were boxes of papers everywhere and I had no idea where to start. Boxes appeared filled with random items Paul was dealing with on a particular day or week; junk mail, coupons, reference material for an article he was working on, stamps, cards, pens, and copies of old newspapers where his different articles had been published. That was his chaotic filing system.

On the Thursday after Paul's death, my son and I spent all day sorting through the junk mail and the piles of papers on the floor, sofa, chairs and tables. We found invoices, money order receipts and financial statements. I also found important tax information in his mother's bedroom. I had to step carefully over piles and piles of bags, boxes and breakables on the floor to get to the bed where I found stacks of older financial statements. I soon learned that Paul didn't have a check book anywhere, just dozens of money order receipts to pay the bills. I was baffled trying to understand his reason for not having a checking account. I couldn't find any invoices of recent bills either, only scattered hints of invoices that had been paid. He had written names or initials and phone numbers on the backs of envelopes near his phone and didn't even have an address book.

"Mom, looks like you're going to have to be a detective to track everything down," my son said.

"Do I need this?" I shook my head. "It's ridiculous."

I started to gather some notes together in order to write his eulogy and obituary for a specific newspaper, which I needed to have ready by that Sunday, alerting people of his death and upcoming memorial. I wasn't sure who knew about his sudden death, so we made sure to send the obituary to several newspapers. I also needed a recent photo of Paul, but my mind was so scattered I couldn't remember where I had any pictures of he and I together. Luckily, I found one of him taken at the gym, on his dining room table. It wasn't a good likeness of him because he wasn't smiling, but I was running out of time and couldn't waste hours scrounging around the house looking for a better picture of him. I would make a black and white portrait vignette for the newspapers by using Photoshop to remove the background gym equipment. My skills as a photo-restoration artist would come in handy.

I went to a local florist and picked out some spring flowers: daises, tulips, mums and wildflowers in red, yellow and black - Germany's national colors. The arrangements would flank a small stone "casket" on the church altar that would symbolize Paul's remains, as they would already be on their way out west. On Saturday, I arranged with Joan Castor to take Paul's cats. She and her husband weren't too thrilled about suddenly adding more cats to a household that already included four of them, but Paul had willed them his pets and they were being well compensated. Ray finally left his set of keys to the house on Friday night since the cats would be gone the following day.

"Can't we just keep one?" Chris asked.

The cats were adorable, but my emphatic "No" was enough for him not to ask again. "They are going to a good home."

—⁂—

On the Tuesday before the memorial, I saw the lawyer and handed him the legal forms the funeral director had given me that he needed to transport Paul's remains on the plane. I introduced my son Chris to Jeff and we gave him a progress report on the house.

"I'm sorry I'm not going to be able to make the memorial," Jeff said. "I promise to send you a picture of the area on the mountain where I spread Paul's ashes."

"The house is really a mess," I said. "When you get back from Colorado I think you should take a look at it."

I set up an appointment with the church's female Reverend, Pastor McAllen. Paul was not a member of the church, but had spent many happy hours giving historical lectures to their retirement club. Pastor McAllen had presided over Mrs. Jaeger's memorial service and he considered her a good friend. We arranged a very old world type of service, European in flavor with some strong German hymns and music. I chose Albrecht Durer's "Praying Hands" as the design on the prayer cards and a soaring eagle flying over mountains as the cover illustration for the memorial program. Both seemed appropriate.

A good friend of mine volunteered to pick up pastries, and I ordered fruit and cheese platters, liquid refreshments and paper supplies for the memorial's noon reception. I designed a poster with an anthropological theme in honor of Paul's profession, and made a collage of the beautiful flower photos he had taken in his garden that spring. He was so proud of the five hundred daffodil bulbs he'd planted. His garden was a visual delight for all his neighbors. Once the posters came back from the printers, I framed both pieces. I planned to place them on matching easels. My artwork and his photos would be on display during his memorial, in a side room, at a time set up for me to meet and greet before the formal service. I picked out a few statues from Paul's vast collection, the faux marble bust of the Veiled Lady and several angels that I thought would make a nice visual display.

In the middle of all this activity, I went to my doctor for some routine blood work and something very strange happened. I parked my station wagon in the rear parking lot of the doctor's office and made certain to push the inside lock on the driver's side door to lock all four doors. I always do this automatically, but I remembered checking the back door handle to be sure, which I normally don't do. I was only in the doctor's office for about fifteen minutes and when I came back to the car, I found the driver's side door slightly ajar. All four locks on the car's doors were open. *What the...* I thought to myself. I became alarmed and looked around. All was quiet. There were expensive cars on either side of my 20-year-old station wagon. What would anyone want with my old car anyway?

I don't keep anything valuable in my car, but I still checked to see if anything had been touched or moved. Everything seemed to be in the same place, including the box of tissues and my eyeglass case. I found it strange that the driver's side door didn't look like it had been forced open and the window wasn't down. A key was needed to open the driver's side door and the only way to unlock all the doors at once was to click the lock inside located in the middle of the door. I debated alerting the doctor's office staff about a possible break-in, but I really didn't want to waste time for them to call the police. Nothing was missing and there was no damage to the car. After thinking about it for another moment, I decided to go home, got into the driver's seat and put the key in the ignition. As I did, I noticed that my dashboard clock read 9:35 AM, the exact time I learned that Paul was gravely ill, exactly one week ago. I just sat there staring at the clock. What was happening? I felt a sudden chill in the warm interior of my car and a sudden wave of sadness swept over me.

I started to tear up. "Ok, Paul, is it you?" I don't know why I said it.

When I got home, I told my son what had happened and he agreed that it was a strange coincidence.

Two days later a second weird coincidence happened, this one at my house.

That morning Chris had just come into the kitchen looking for some breakfast.

"You want some hot chocolate?" I asked him.

As we stood by the kitchen sink, we heard a scraping and rattling noise and then a sound like something had fallen. We went into the living room and found that an item from Paul's American Indian souvenirs, which I had been granted in the will, had toppled over. The 8 inch piece of slate with an Indian petroglyph engraved on it had a small chip missing from one side. Chris and I looked at each other.

"It's Paul!" We both said and laughed.

"Maybe when I walked by the fireplace on my way into the kitchen the vibrations jarred it loose," Chris said.

I looked it over again and knew that it had been wedged firmly against a piece of side molding so what Chris was saying was impossible. We also knew from the sounds it hadn't just fallen over. There had definitely been a rattling noise before it fell over. I didn't want to draw any conclusions, but Paul knew something like that would get my attention.

—⁓—

The memorial on Thursday, January 29 went smoothly, with about 40 people in attendance. Paul would have been gratified to see so many people there on a weekday, braving the cold temperatures, with ice and snow on the ground. Many came out of respect for Paul's contributions to the community, including the many anthropological and historical lectures he'd given and the articles he'd written for the Community Focus, a local paper, over the years. Pastor McAllen gave a heartfelt talk about Paul. I gave the eulogy.

"I want to welcome everyone and thank you for coming in such inclement weather. I think Paul would be really happy and gratified to see you all here. I want to thank my family and friends for all their love and support this past week and especially my son, Chris, for all his help. I want to express my sincerest condolences to the Jaeger family and especially Carl, for the loss of his brother, Paul."

I took a deep breath and continued. "How do you write a eulogy for a writer? I have to confess that after I wrote this my first instinct was to show it to Paul."

The audience's laugher at this poignant moment eased my nerves and I knew I'd be able to get through the entire eulogy I had written. Everyone gave me his undivided attention during my reading. Finally, I gave my concluding remarks. "He is going to be sorely missed in the writing and cultural communities and his colleagues are still stunned by his sudden death.

Leonard Bernstein wrote, '*to achieve great things, two things are needed: a plan and not quite enough time.*' We will always wonder why he left us so soon, but Paul did achieve much in his lifetime.

Paul Jaeger was a true Renaissance man and we all are going to miss his immense talent, his great company and friendship. He was truly one of a kind. I felt privileged to know him and to call him my friend. He will live in our hearts and memories for years to come - so he'll never be really gone." I paused a moment. "One last thing I'd like to read is from an inscription on a tombstone that Paul had photographed in a cemetery that I found among his pictures. It reads:

If tears could build a stairway, and memories a lane,
I'd walk right up to Heaven and bring you home again.

Auf Wiedersehen, Paul." I then blew him a kiss towards heaven.

Carl surprised us all by wanting to speak briefly about his brother, but didn't say anything out of line and I was greatly relieved. He came without Doris, but brought his son and daughter instead. He shook hands with me briefly and introduced them. I found them very polite and cordial. They were good-looking kids and I learned they both had nice families, decent jobs and were successful in their lives. Paul had completely detached himself from them and had missed their lives for many years. It was indeed a shame.

That evening I was finally able to look inside the bag from Springfield Hospital that contained Paul's personal belongings. I was touched to see a folded piece of paper with my name and phone number in his wallet, 'contact in case of emergency'. Inside were his eyeglasses, asthma inhaler, deodorant, pen and notepad. I suddenly felt exhausted; it had been such an emotional day. Flopping down on my bed, I let out a long sigh. I had done all that was required of me to put him to rest and to honor his memory and had little time to grieve these last few days. Now with these few personal items in my hands, the reality hit me and I began to cry, rocking back and forth, holding his glasses close to me. That brilliant mind was gone forever. He would never again look through his glasses to research or write another article. I would never talk to him on the phone again or have one of our marathon conversations on history. I would never hear one of his witty, silly jokes that only he and I got. He was gone and I was in charge of the remains of his life that he so abruptly left behind. What was I to do next?

Chapter 5

THE BIG CLEAN-UP

My son and I spent the Saturday after the memorial forming a plan on what we would do next at the house.

It was a one-story ranch with three bedrooms, a bath, small kitchen, living room and dining room, enclosed porch in front of the house and a side "summer porch" off the kitchen. The property also included a detached 2-car garage with attic and a small masonry garden house.

These outside structures were also filled to the brim with stuff Paul and his family hoarded for the last thirty years. Not only did I have to go through all of the accumulated junk, but also there were important documents, family heirlooms, collectable dolls, plates, statues, photos, and paintings, hundreds of music tapes and videos, all specified in a detailed seven-page will. Also listed were forty-three separate items that had to be identified that he left to specific people or organizations. We had to separate items into distinct classes: what went to his brother and his family, what went to people in his will, what would be donated, what had to be thrown out, what to keep and research later, and what he had willed to me.

Getting the house cleaned out was going to be a huge challenge. It was going to be a difficult task, to say the least.

The lawyer's advice had been to hire a cleaning crew to help with the work, but I told him no. I had no idea what was in the hundreds of boxes, bags, and bins and I did not intend to have strangers, paid by the hour, looking over my shoulder while I went through them.

"I think it would be a good idea if Chris helped me instead," I offered.

"That would probably work out better," Jeff said. "I think I can arrange for the estate to pay him an hourly wage as long as he keeps invoices with an honest tally of the hours he worked. I don't think there will be a problem."

"Good," I said. "I need someone I can trust and I know I can trust my son."

It was going to be convenient for Chris to help me, too, since his hours at his job as a multi-media technician, were cut back dramatically since the beginning of the year. My business was going to be impacted as well by the amount of time I'd be spending at the house. I learned I wasn't allowed to charge a fee for my services because I would be compensated as the executrix in the end. When it was all over, I would spend well over eleven hundred hours of my time on Paul's estate. I realized that no amount of money would ever get me do it again.

I hadn't gone into Paul's basement after his death because he'd told me on numerous occasions that he had cleaned it up and since there had been so much to do on the first floor, I almost forgot about it. We decided it was time to check it out. As I started down the dimly lit stairs, I saw a sea of papers ahead of me, and piles of stuff scattered everywhere. There were two-foot piles of magazines on each step, and with such poor lighting I had to be careful on my way down the stairs not to trip.

I stopped half way down the steps and surveyed the rest of the basement from the open sides of the railings. I had no idea the basement was so big! It was open in the front and divided into two large rooms by a wooden partition with shelves in the back of the staircase.

I stepped down on the concrete basement floor and its surface was covered entirely with piles of junk, clothes, newspapers and suitcases. There were hundreds of plastic bins and cardboard boxes stacked floor to ceiling, cabinets and shelves overflowing with books and magazines, pictures, and posters, not to mention the fifteen wardrobes and closets filled with clothes, coats, sweaters, hats and shoes. The shelves, packed with small appliances, went up to the ceiling.

"Are you kidding me?" I cried. *Christ, Paul, you told me you'd cleaned up this place and how proud you were and I believed you!* "You lying son of a bitch," I said under my breath. "God forgive me for speaking ill of the dead."

The sight was so shocking I started to cry.

Chris came down the steps. "Holy shit, look at this place!"

I turned to him. "Can you believe this? How am I going to go through all this?"

Chris put his hand on my shoulder. "It's ok, Mom, we'll do it one day at a time, one pile at a time."

That night I couldn't sleep with the thoughts that kept racing through my head. The burden was almost too much to bear. *Oh, Paul how could you die and leave all this on me?*

—⁂—

On Sunday morning, my girlfriend Rose called and asked how I'd been holding up. She also asked if I'd like her to bring over some lunch and I gladly responded in the affirmative. She gave me a big hug when she came to the door and told me again what a great job I'd done with the memorial and eulogy. As we ate lunch, Chris and I talked about the house and the smelly basement.

"Can I see the house sometime?" Rose asked.

Rose had known Paul for as long as I had and she had been to his house so I thought it would be fine if she came with us that afternoon. As we entered the house, she couldn't believe how awful it smelled.

She looked around and sighed deeply. "I can't believe this," she said. "Paul must have been in real trouble."

"It was a shock to me too when I first saw it," I said

The kitchen still looked dirty and cluttered, as I'd had scant time to give it a good cleaning. We had been concentrating on clearing out the papers on the tables and on the floor and throwing out rotten food. After a brief look around the house, we took some pictures for the lawyer, and went down to the basement. I thought Rose was going to have a heart attack. She stood at the bottom of the stairs just staring at the mess. Her mouth was open in astonishment.

"Oh, my God, Anita, this is the worst. How could he have let it get this bad? My God, it's unbelievable."

"Yes, I know, you see it, but you don't believe it," I said.

We carefully walked around and took a good look. It was the first time I had been able to do so and I found it much worse than my first impression. The place looked ransacked. The smell was just terrible. It reeked of mold, stale air, dust, mildew and camphor.

"Are you guys aware of how dangerous this mold is?" Rose asked when she saw an ugly black rim on the concrete wall near the washer. "This place must have had flooding for a long time."

She was right. This discussion had come up many times with Paul. He would tell me he'd had water in the basement, but had always managed to clean it up with a small pump and a Shop Vac. I remember asking him why he didn't have a trench dug with a sump pump installed but he always changed the subject. He never really addressed the problem because he didn't consider it serious. *He always had money to travel to Europe,* I thought as I stood there looking at the mess in the basement.

"No wonder he had asthma," Rose said. "This has to be one of the unhealthiest environments I've ever seen. How could he live this way? I can't stand the smell anymore."

With that, she quickly headed for the stairs.

"It's so unbelievable. How do you expect to handle this, Anita? Does the lawyer know what condition this place is in?" She began to tear up and cough into a tissue.

I put my hand on her arm. "I really appreciate your concern, but we're going to take every precaution. We're going to buy more rubber work gloves, masks, disinfectant and as many trash bags as we need."

Rose sighed. "Please be careful, you guys. That place will make you both sick."

Later, she told me that when she got home that night she could hardly sleep with the image of Paul's house in her mind and the job ahead of me, and worried about how dangerous that environment was to us. She was very upset. The combination of her mother's death and Paul's recent death and the way he had lived had a strong effect on her. The next day she called a clean-up crew to come and take away the junk in her basement, made plans to have her sump pump updated, the basement floor and walls sealed from mold and repainted and ordered new plastic shelving. This was something she'd wanted to do for a long time and seeing Paul's house motivated her into getting it done.

That same Sunday night Chris had a chilling dream. When he came downstairs the next morning, he said he wasn't hungry and went directly to his worktable in the living room. He stood over a model miniature he'd been painting and began to work on it again. He had been painting Warhammer models for over twelve years and was an excellent model builder and painter.

I was at the dining room table paying some bills.

"It's not a good idea to skip breakfast," I said.

Chris looked at me. "I'll have an early lunch."

Looking through all of Paul's bills that were now being forwarded to me, I didn't know where to start, and soon became lost in concentration. I glanced over to my son once or twice and knowing him so well, felt he was being unusually quiet. Something was bothering him.

"Is something wrong, Chris?"

Chris didn't look up. He was silent for a moment and then, as if trying to find the right phrasing he said, "By the way, Paul says 'Hi.'"

Surprised, I stopped what I was doing and looked up at him. "What are you talking about?"

My son still had his head bent over the model and was deep in concentration. "I saw Paul last night in a dream that really didn't feel like a dream. It was very vivid. He was sitting across from me on the recliner in our living room dressed in a red hoodie and dark brown pants. He told me he was at the memorial service and that you'd done a great job. He really liked it."

I just stared at Chris.

"He also said to me that a massive cleanup seemed to be underway at his house and he was saddened that things were being changed."

35

I was stunned. "Are you kidding me?"

"No, I'm not kidding, Mom. Paul's face looked gray and he told me that he'd been a bit scattered lately and it had taken a while for him to get his energy back."

I couldn't believe what I was hearing because it sounded just like Paul to use a pun like 'being scattered' when he knew full well that his last wishes were to have his ashes scattered on a mountain top, as they had been only days earlier.

I guess I was feeling a little hurt that my friend hadn't come to me. "I wonder why he came to you and not me," I said.

"He came to me because he knows how mad you are at him. He figured you didn't want to see him."

I put my hand to my mouth. "Oh my God!"

Chris continued, "He seemed to think like there was nothing wrong in his mind, and that it was business as usual and that he was going home after our visit. Then, he said, 'I'll see you again,' and I told him, 'Dude, you're dead.' He didn't say anything; he just got up from the chair and walked right through the wall."

My jaw dropped.

"Mom, I feel so drained this morning, like I didn't get any sleep at all last night."

"I don't know what to say Chris," as chills ran up my spine. Then I had a creepy thought. *Of course, Paul's complexion looked gray; he had been cremated, hadn't he?*

Chapter 6

A SICK HOUSE

We first realized that something else besides the hoarding wasn't right at the house on a cold Saturday morning in February. We didn't like being there during the weekend since we spent so much time there during the week, but Paul's elderly neighbor, Barbara, had called me the night before and told me that a tree limb had fallen on his roof and she didn't know if there was any damage. I had seen her at Paul's memorial and I knew how much she missed him, as he'd been like a son to her.

"I'll miss his smile the most," she had said to me.

We also went that day to check the roof gutters. We'd been getting water in the basement and the gutters looked clogged. I called someone I knew and asked him if he could clean them out. I wanted to see what he had done since I hadn't been there the day he came to do the job.

I looked up at the roof. "It looks good for now, but it's only a temporary fix."

We went behind the house to check on the large tree limb and fortunately, it was only half on the roof. Chris was able to grab it and pull it onto the ground.

When I entered the house, it seemed unusually chilly. I walked into the living room to check on the thermostat and thought I heard three distinct moans coming from below in the basement. Since Chris came into the room after I did, he only heard the last moan.

"That's creepy," he said. "Why is it so cold in here? Is the heat working?"

It's fine, I just checked it," I said. When we weren't there, I kept the heat at 63 degrees. "It feels like there's a cold draft just in this part of the room."

We listened for a few moments, but didn't hear anything else. The rest of the room felt warmer than the one spot we had walked through. We waited a little more, still wondering what had caused the noises and hoped it was something easily explained. "Maybe the noises are coming from outside," Chris said, trying to be reasonable.

I shrugged. "I don't know." I couldn't pinpoint where the sound was coming from. "Let's check the basement."

We went downstairs and put several small towels on the floor to sop up a small pool of water that had appeared due to the recent runoff of melting snow.

"I hope that having the gutters fixed takes care of the water problems for now," I said. We didn't need to have more moisture on top of the mold problem we already had.

"Let's go, Mom," Chris said. "The smell down here is giving me a headache."

That wasn't the first time Chris mentioned feeling sick or having a headache while at the house. We took our precautions with filter masks, rubber gloves and wore clothing to cover up our arms and legs, but Chris still got sick. Sometimes he would start feeling nauseated or lightheaded in the car, blocks away from the house, and had constant stuffiness and sinus problems. On more than one occasion, he had to go to the doctor for medication. At other times, it affected his stomach and he'd go running to the bathroom, or he had to run outside to vomit. The smell was that bad. Once he'd leave the house and go home, he'd feel better.

I didn't seem to be affected as much as he was but, in reality, we didn't know how much we were being injured by what we were being exposed to. I have to credit my son's endurance for sticking it out with me. In the beginning, he had told me he couldn't let me go through it alone and he had kept his word. Although, it helped him out financially, he wasn't doing it for the money. He was doing it out of love and loyalty for me. We were determined to do our job, but we were both spending time in a very unhealthy and potentially dangerous environment and that worried me.

—∾—

It wasn't all drudgery, though. We had moments of fun and excitement finding treasures in the trash. My son started calling me "History Queen," the on-site history expert. He would hold up some obscure item and ask me what it was and most of the time I could look at, and identify, it. I had earned a B.S. in Art Education and had been a teacher, and now I had a business as a photo, painting and doll restoration artist and having a near photographic memory came in handy.

"You may not have a Master's Degree in Anthropology, but you are just as knowledgeable about the field as I am," Paul had once said to me. I thought it was the highest compliment he ever paid me.

"That's a Mayan carved relief," I said to my son after he showed me one of the artifacts he found, or "No, that's not a junky stone, that's an American Indian scraper tool."

"A what?"

Once Chris held up a signed autograph picture and held it up for me to see. "That's a picture of Grace Kelly," I said.

"Who?" Chris asked.

"You don't know her, but trust me, keep it."

"You know, Mom, you were born for this job."

Box after box would yield one surprise after another. One funny incident happened in the basement when my son grabbed a black trash bag and was ready to throw it out, but couldn't make out what was in it.

"I think it's a Viking helmet, Mom, I feel horns."

I stopped what I was doing in another part of the basement. "A Viking helmet? Let me see?" I asked.

I took the bag from my son and found another brown bag inside that contained something and I felt the outline of horns. I opened it and was surprised.

"Oh, cool, it's a Plains Indian Shaman Headdress," I said. "These are buffalo horns. Shoot, it looks like the tip is broken off one horn but the piece is still there. Just look at the intricate beadwork on the headband. Wow, I wonder where he got it?"

Chris rolled his eyes at me. "Yeah, it looks pretty ratty to me. It would have been cool if it was a Viking helmet."

"And you almost threw it out," I said as I put it on top of the "keep" pile.

That was our constant dilemma. We had to search every bag even if it looked like trash because we never knew what we were going to find. It took a tremendous amount of time and we had no choice but to conduct it like an archaeology dig. It was tedious work but well worth it when I was able to find every single item mentioned in Paul's will that was to go to his family, to me and his other friends. How ironic it all was; as an anthropologist, he had gone on archaeology digs in the American southwest and in South America, and now I was conducting an expedition in his own house. I guess the joke was on me.

Chapter 7

PHANTOM PHONE CALLS

After I started paying the bills for Paul's house, I noticed something odd about the phone bill. When I reviewed March's phone bill there was a strange number that showed up under long distance calls. It was a number to Bethlehem, Pennsylvania, and the calls came from Paul's house at precisely 4:05 AM once a week, always on the same day. MCI was charging us per call for a minute, which meant a connection went through.

Intrigued, I rechecked February's bill and saw four charges for the same exact number. I called the lawyer's office and his assistant, Linda tried to find some information about the number, but was unable to.

"When did the calls start, Anita?"

I again looked over the February bill and saw what I missed. I couldn't believe it. The first time the odd phone number appeared was on January 29, the day of Paul's memorial.

Then I contacted MCI and they said the calls were definitely coming from his house to that number. However, we had discontinued long distance service. How was this possible?

"Is there a fax machine or another phone line there?" they asked.

"No," I said. "He only had one phone, wasn't computer savvy, and didn't own a fax machine or answering machine. He only had caller ID."

"I never heard of such a thing." The phone representative said. "It's very strange. The only thing you can do is see if the calls continue for the next few months."

As a courtesy, they removed the charges. From then on, I went over the phone bill carefully each month and the weird phone calls continued every week on the same day at the same time. We called the number and the phone rang far away in the distance. Finally, it sounded like the receiver was automatically picked up and then the line would go dead. This went on until we changed phone providers in June. Then, the calls stopped. We never found out whose number it was or why the phone dialed to that number. Was Paul telling me that 4:05 AM was when his spirit left his physical body and departed the earthly plane?

Chapter 8

WHERE'S MY STUFF?

It was March 19 and it was time to take the dozens of Egyptian, Greek, Roman and Mayan statues out of Paul's room and pack them in the plastic crates we had taken from the basement. Since they were all going to me, I labeled them and packed them for storage. For a couple of minutes, Chris watched me as I did this.

"How do you feel about taking all his stuff?" he asked.

I looked at him. "I'm not sure. I didn't realize I was inheriting a museum. It's like each piece represents a small part of Paul."

During that week, we continued to go through hundreds of artifacts, statues and books related to anthropology. We had to walk single file to Paul's bed because there were things piled everywhere.

We also had to do something with the bedroom furniture. I called his brother, Carl, who was now on speaking terms with me, to ask him if he wanted it, even though it looked old and worn. He said yes. I later learned it was part of his parent's first bedroom set.

Chris was busy going through and emptying one of the dresser drawers when he came across a figurine wrapped in plastic.

"It looks like a doll, Mom," he said.

I took it from him and looked at it through the plastic wrap.

"No," I said. "It looks like a figurine of Scarlett O'Hara."

"Here's another part of it," Chris said and handed me what looked like a staircase wrapped in plastic.

I examined it closely. "It's a music box and I think the two pieces fit together with Scarlett descending the staircase. How pretty," I said.

I put the two separately wrapped pieces on the dresser when suddenly the musical theme from *Gone with the Wind* began to play. Then something that looked to be a gold flash of light appeared out of nowhere and flew between us and we heard a loud bang. We looked at each other in shock; we couldn't see anything that had fallen.

"I'm done, Mom, I'm out of here," Chris said.

Uncomfortable and puzzled by the strange things that just happened, we wanted to get out of the house as quickly as we could. We went to Paul's mother's bedroom to take out the trash and weren't there more than five minutes when we heard a loud crash come from Paul's room.

"Jesus!" I yelled as we headed back in that direction. "It sounds like the entire bookcase came down."

We found that the three large plastic Tupperware bins that had been stacked against the back wall of his room had toppled over on the floor, their lids popped off and their contents spilled onto the middle of the floor. They appeared to have been violently pushed over from the back wall to the center of the room.

"I think Paul is mad that we're taking all of his stuff," Chris said.

Was that it? I was startled, tired and didn't know what to do. I looked around at the mountain of work ahead of us and tried to think of a way to calm the ghost of my dead friend. I wiped a tear from my eye with my shirtsleeve.

"Paul, if it's you, I'm sorry. Do you know that you're dead? You died weeks ago and I'm only doing what you asked me to do in your will. I have to pack all of your things so I can sell the house. Please, give me a break!"

We waited and things did settle down. Chris and I picked up the mess and left for the day. Later that night, I checked the *Gone with the Wind* music box and removed the bubble wrap from the base only to see there was a small button you had to slide to one side in order for it to start playing. Therefore, it hadn't started to play because I had picked it up. How in the world had it played on its own?

—∞—

Paul once told me in a phone conversation that if anything happened to him he would try and get in touch with me after his death.

"That's a bit morbid, Paul," I had said. "Let's get off the subject."

That happened a few months after his beloved mother died and we had been discussing theology in general. We both had problems with established organized religion, even though we'd both been raised in conventional Christian religions. We were in a quest for answers to eternal questions and found that our mutual study of anthropology gave us a wide scope to explore other religions and their views on the after-life. We both tended to be more spiritual than religious.

"No, really, I believe my Mom has been in touch with me here at the house," Paul said.

I listened to his explanation and I believed him. "You were so close to your Mom, Paul, and she knew how much you loved her and took care of her. Maybe she's just letting you know that she was grateful for all you did and she's watching over you."

I heard him choke back the tears. "Anita, promise me that if something happens to me, you won't be afraid if I contact you."

"Ok," I said. Now I was choking up. "God, what are we talking about? We have so many years ahead of us."

"Promise me, Anita."

"Okay, okay, if something happens to me first, Paul, I'll try and get in touch with you."

We got off the subject and never talked about our "pact" again. Was he now trying to keep his promise to me?

Chapter 9

LOCKED IN

Because of the adverse conditions in the basement, it meant that only a limited number of people were willing to help us. Those who did had to join us in wearing masks, protective gloves and old clothes and shoes. Who could blame them for not wanting to help?

"Do you think we'll have the house cleaned up in nine months, a year or a year and half?" the lawyer asked us a few months into the cleanup.

I had to laugh because it wasn't like he was doing any of the work. At the rate we were going, with thirty hours of work on site that turned into more like forty hours a week for me with all the paperwork, phone calls and bills to pay, we were hoping for the nine month goal. We had serious doubts that we would be able to get everything done in that amount of time, but felt it was doable if we didn't have too many distractions and didn't run into any new problems. Then, Murphy's Law geared up on us.

—⁓—

Tuesday, May 26th

"Whatayadoin Danny?" my son asked in his best Tony Soprano voice as he turned around to look at his friend.

We were in my car making our way to the house and Danny's phone kept making a weird beeping noise. We had been spending many hours at the house lately and my old blue station wagon was once again loaded with boxes that we would use for packing. The annoying beeping went for a few minutes until Danny finally looked up from the phone.

"Huh?" he said.

Danny worked as a waiter and was a good kid with a short build and a buzz haircut. He had a slight case of ADD and his mind tended to wander so you had to keep reminding him to stay focused on one thing at a time. Nevertheless, he was a loyal friend to Chris and a very funny and upbeat person. He didn't have to go to work until later that night so he volunteered to help us out at the house. I asked my son if I should pay him for his time.

Chris shook his head. "Just bribe him with the chicken corn chowder soup from WAWA. My friends and I can't get enough of it."

After we stopped to pick up lunch, Chris and Danny kept talking about how much they couldn't wait to eat the soup.

"Come on guys, it can't be *that* good," I said.

"Have you had it?" they both asked.

Taking a break to eat good food also served as a release valve for the constant pressure we felt we were under all the time. It had taken my son and me almost four months to clear out half the basement and we still had a problem with flooding. I convinced the lawyer that it was time that we commissioned a water proofing company to construct a sump pump system.

The company scheduled Thursday, May 28, for the construction work, and that meant we had to clear out a forty-five foot section of the back wall. There were still boxes stacked to the ceiling, and back shelves filled with God-knows-what that had to be sorted and piled on the other side of the basement. The crew would be putting up plastic sheets to protect the rest of the basement from all the dirt and dust that the jackhammers would cause.

This was a big job and I was glad Danny was there to help. We took a break for lunch and Chris said he had to use the bathroom. Danny and I followed Chris upstairs to a bedroom right near the bathroom. I had a bag of trash to put out, which Danny promptly grabbed and took outside. I was in the kitchen getting our sandwiches when I heard Chris yell. Danny was just coming into the kitchen when I heard Chris scream for a second time. "Let me out!"

We ran quickly to the bathroom where Chris was banging on the door.

"The door knob won't turn. It's frozen, I'm locked in!" He sounded frantic.

"Hold on, Chris," I said, my heart pounding furiously. "I'll try the door knob."

I grabbed the doorknob, expecting the worst. Surprisingly, it turned easily and the door opened. My son bound out the door, sweating profusely.

"I didn't close the door all the way when I went into the bathroom," he explained. "It just closed on me."

Danny agreed. "When I walked by I saw that you didn't have the door closed all the way."

We tested the doorknob and it turned easily.

"I don't know what happened," Chris said and quickly changed the subject. "Man, I'm starving."

"Ok, who wants some chicken corn chowder soup and flat bread sandwiches?" I asked.

We sat at the table and began to eat. "Oh, man this soup is to die for," Danny said.

"After what just happened, I think we could phrase that differently, Danny," I said.

We all had a good laugh and were able to relax for the moment.

Little did we know at this time that moments of relaxation would be few and far between the more time we spent at Paul's house.

After I finished lunch, I had to admit that the soup was *really* good.

Chapter 10

POLTERGEIST ACTIVITY

May 27th

The next day we got to the house around 11 A.M. My boyfriend Bob had offered to help and we were expecting him to join us around noon. While we were working in the basement, we thought we heard his footsteps in the living room above.

I called out. "Bob?" There was no answer. I went upstairs to an empty room. There was no one there.

Fifteen minutes later Bob arrived at the side porch door. "Reporting for duty," he joked, his blue eyes twinkling.

He helped me to pack up some glasses. We were so busy working that we weren't paying close attention to the sounds of things being dropped.

"What keeps falling?" I asked Chris, who was on the other side of the steps and had heard the sound too.

"It sounds like something hit the work bench," he said.

"How can you tell?" I said. "There's so much crap on top of it." I went back to work.

A few seconds later, we heard a sound. Ting!

"What was that?" I asked.

Chris walked over to the workbench and saw a metal pen on the floor. Being able to see the pen meant that the floor was clean—all due to our hard work. The sound, of whatever thrown, could no longer be muffled by the countless objects that had littered the basement floor.

"I think this pen was thrown," my son said as he picked it up and showed it to me.

We both stopped what we were doing and listened. Bang! We looked around, but it was impossible to pinpoint where the thing had landed. All we knew was that something unexplainable was happening—again. Bob came down the steps after unloading trash bags and asked what was going on.

"There's stuff being thrown around."

He looked at me skeptically

"I'm serious, Bob," I said

He looked around the room. "What else is going up?" he asked.

He went upstairs again. Out of the corner of my eye, I watched a book fly off the shelf and I picked it up and laughed when I saw the title, *The Story of the von Trapp Family Singers*. Knowing the connection between Paul and Maria von Trapp I felt strongly that he might be trying to contact me.

"Ooo-kay, a cassette tape just flew right by me and smashed against the wall," Chris said.

"Let me see," I said.

Bob was still upstairs and hadn't seen or heard what just happened. When I walked to the bottom of the stairs to see if Bob was coming down, a black object flashed by the side of my face and I screamed.

Chris ran over to me, concerned. "What is it, Mom?" he asked.

"I don't know. It was a black blur." My heart was racing. I looked around the floor and spotted a black glove not far from my feet. "That's what it was."

Whoever or whatever was throwing these objects around seemed to have plenty of things to choose from and was having fun distracting us from what we were supposed to be doing. At that moment, I saw Bob coming down the steps. He stopped abruptly as a white streak whizzed past him, right in front of his face.

Plunk! It landed in the plastic bin at the bottom of the steps. I looked inside the bin and Bob scratched his head, apparently still skeptical

"It's a sea shell," I said, holding it up for Bob to see.

A white music cassette tape suddenly flew from the shelf near the steps and crashed, hitting the wall twenty feet away from us.

"Now do you believe that there's something strange going on down here, Bob?" I yelled. I immediately apologized to him but the tension in the basement was high.

Chris looked at Bob. "Have you ever seen the movie, *Poltergeist?*" He asked. "What's happening here is just like what happened in that movie. Something invisible is moving things around!"

Bob shook his head. "You mean like a ghost? I don't believe in that stuff."

"Haven't you ever watched any of those shows on TV about ghosts?" I asked "You know like *Ghost Hunters.*"

"Once, and it was really bad," Bob said.

"How else can you explain this?" I asked. "We've been working down here for the last four months and suddenly things are now moving on their own all around the room." I was exasperated that Bob was being so narrow-minded. We weren't making this up

"I think we disturbed something," Chris said. "Things were fine down here until we moved all that stuff from the back wall."

I nodded. "You could be right, Chris." Maybe something was trying to distract us from doing what we had to do by tomorrow. The work crew was coming and we had to finish the preparations.

Random objects continued to be thrown for several hours as we worked; a pack of Saint Patrick's Day stickers, more sea shells, a bamboo wooden flute, a small dowel stick, and a Christmas tree light bulb. I don't know how to explain it, but we weren't frightened, as people might think. In fact, we were fascinated. We knew we were witnessing something extraordinary and we tried to take it all in.

Chris looked just in time to see a Santa Claus metal can slide and then fall from a shelf above the workbench.

"Did you see that?" Chris asked. "It moved to the end of the shelf and fell!"

"This is unbelievable," was all I could say.

I came across a photo of a much younger Paul holding his infant nephew. It was a sweet picture, but the faded photo was stuck to the glass and the glass had mold on it. I hated to throw out old photos, but this was disgusting so I tossed it into one of the black trash bags.

It was near the end of the afternoon and Bob had to get back to his ailing mother so we decided to call it quits for the day. Chris put the black trash bag that held the moldy photo near the bottom of the steps. Later, he would remember twisting the top and folding it over to one side. Bob headed for the steps and Chris and I went around the basement putting out lights. When I passed the workbench, I heard a distinct smack on the concrete floor. I walked over to it and saw a small square picture frame face down on the floor.

"Oh, you have to be kidding me," I said.

"What is it, Mom?" Chris asked.

I turned the picture frame over and saw that it was the same picture of Paul and his nephew. "Look," I said and showed it to Chris and Bob.

"That's freaky," Chris said.

"I think it's time to go, guys," Bob said.

We agreed, but first I wanted to put the picture frame back into the trash bag and see what would happen. Bob wasn't amused. As we reached the top step, we heard the familiar slap as something hit the concrete floor. We peered into the darkened basement and could make out a lone object on the floor. The three of us laughed nervously.

Bob held up a paper cup. "If it's that picture frame again, I'll eat this," he said. He was serious.

Slowly, I went down the steps, reached for the basement light and walked to the object on the floor. It wasn't the picture frame, but a woman's small brown leather coin purse. I showed it to Bob, who was relieved that he didn't have to eat the paper cup.

"Where did that come from, Mom?" Chris said.

I laughed. "I don't know, but they're cheap ghosts. There isn't even any money in it."

As I closed the basement door, I thought I heard a small bang, but was not going to investigate any further. *God, I thought, the work crew is coming tomorrow. What's in store for them?*

—⁂—

The following day the work crew arrived to begin the task of breaking up the concrete floor and putting in a trench for a new sump pump. As the first man walked down the steps, I heard him kick something hard with his work boot and it fell to the floor. When I picked it up, I saw it was a large spool of brown sewing thread. It had been sitting on the step waiting for the first person to step on it and I don't know if the intention was to trip someone, but it could have been dangerous. Were the ghosts having the last laugh?

The supervisor directed his crew to start using the jackhammer and one of them joked with me that he would now know "where the bodies were kept." I rolled my eyes at the attempt at construction humor. Climbing the steps, I thought, *that's not funny after what happened yesterday. Let's see if you're still laughing when you get hit with a shovel!*

It was a humid, hot Thursday when the five-man crew dug a trench through the concrete floor, removed the clogged sinks, drains and pipes, and ripped out the old bathroom and wood partition behind the stairs that separated the two sections of the basement. The few small basement windows, ground level and cemented shut offered little light and no ventilation. Buckets of dirt, boxes of debris and splintered sections of moldy wall board and paneling were hauled up manually by the one set of steps leading from the basement through the kitchen and side porch, the only access to the dump trucks in the driveway. After nine brutal hours, they were finished and luckily, the crew completed their dirty job without ghostly incident. We wouldn't share the same luck. In the aftermath, we would discover what paranormal experts mean when they say construction can wake "sleeping" ghosts up!

—※—

The following Monday morning, June 1, Danny came to help us carry a load of cartons from the state store to the house. We made frequent trips to the state store because the boxes were free and they were a good size - not too bulky or too heavy.

We had to pack over eighty boxes of books that Paul had designated for donation to a community library. My son's boss, Kent, had been kind enough to let us borrow the company van to deliver the books. Danny came because he was anxious to see the new drainage system in the basement. On the way over, we told him about the poltergeist activity; he believed us and agreed that something crazy was happening at the house.

"Wow, you guys did a great job! The whole back wall is cleared out," he said.

He walked around the basement, stacking empty boxes. I told him about some of the things thrown around the room, when in the middle of my sentence we all heard a loud clang. Something had hit the floor.

Danny looked up at us wide-eyed. "What was that?"

We looked around us and soon found the lid to a metal can with German writing on it lying on the floor.

"You're kidding me," Danny said and started to laugh.

Chris and I began to laugh with him and told him that this was how things had started the other day.

"Wait, wait," I said. "Let's do this like they do on that show about paranormal hunters? Let's ask a question."

The boys were trying to stifle their laughter.

"Shh...be still," I said. I tried to remain calm but felt excited. "If there are any spirits here, or if it's you Paul, please make a noise or give me a sign."

We held our breath and within fifteen seconds, we heard a bang against a metal locker that was only ten feet away from us.

"Let's get the hell out of here!" Danny said.

Chris looked shocked. I walked over to the metal cabinet and saw a photo slide on the ground. It had a cardboard fitting, but it had hit the metal door of the locker hard. I held up the slide to the light, and saw a man in colonial attire with knee breeches and vest standing near a printing press. I looked at the writing on the cardboard and it was a slide from Williamsburg, Virginia. I immediately remembered that I had seen a black and white photo of Paul dressed in the same type of outfit taken at Ben Franklin's Printing Shop. One summer Paul had worked for the Philadelphia Bicentennial as a tour guide and often wore colonial outfits for work. I remember him telling me how much fun he had with his job and going into the city every day. He had been one of the tour guides for Queen Elizabeth on her Bicentennial visit to Philadelphia.

"It's Paul," I said. "He just gave me a sign."

The boys didn't wait for more explanations and went flying up the stairs. I looked up at them at the top of the landing.

"Ah, come on, Paul would never hurt us," I said.

"We're fine up here, Mom," Chris said.

I continued my experiment. "Let's make sure. I'll try one more time." I spoke once again to the unseen entity, "If that was you Paul, let me know again. Please make a noise."

Within seconds, I heard a loud clang and looked down at the concrete floor. Near my feet, I saw a religious medal with a relief sculptured Madonna on it. It was the type of medal that Catholics put on the visors of their cars for spiritual protection. I picked it up and it was hot to the touch.

"See, it is him!" I said triumphantly holding up the medal and looking up at them.

Danny suddenly made the sign of the cross. "Goodbye," he said.

He and Chris ran out the kitchen door to the car as fast as they could.

Chapter 11

SPOOKY SPECTERS

June 10th

As the weeks progressed, we faced a major problem - what to do with the more than fifteen wardrobes in the basement filled with coats, jackets, sweaters and suits. In each wardrobe were hundreds of items that had belonged to Paul's mother. I had no idea that she had hoarded so much in her life and Paul's refusal to part with any of it since her death eight years earlier was quite a surprise.

On this particular day, after several hours upstairs in the house, my son and I decided it was time to go through the summer clothes so a local charity could donate them to families who were in desperate need of clothing. It was around 11:00 AM. Bob had just come over to help us.

That morning I had let in the service man to check the heater and air conditioning units and perform the annual tune-ups and cleaning of their filters. He had known Paul for several years and was surprised he wasn't there to greet him. I introduced myself and told him why I was there.

"That's too bad, he was a nice man. I'm so sorry to hear of his passing," he said. "Don't worry about the heating or the air conditioning. He had a contract with our company for annual inspections. This shouldn't take long."

He began to work. Bob and I decided to tackle the eight foot long canvas and plastic zip-up wardrobes that hung by metal hooks to poles in the ceiling. We got into a rhythm, with me taking out each piece of clothing, checking its condition, sorting it for summer wear and depositing it in the bag Bob was holding.

Chris was sitting not far from us where he was opening another plastic tub that he called "a box of surprises." I had asked him to fill a box for Paul's brother of anything related to their German heritage, as well as one for pictures, one for collectibles and one for important papers, if he found any.

With this system in place, we were able to get through several hundred items in an hour. Bob and I were just filling up another black trash bag when I heard Chris say, "Where did these come from?"

Bob and I walked over to him. "What's up?' I asked.

Chris pointed to a small stack of black and white pictures scattered off to the left of him, near his chair. "They weren't there a minute ago," he said.

"Are you sure they didn't come from one of the boxes you just emptied out?" I asked

"No," Chris said. "If I find any photos they go directly into this box." He pointed to a large shoebox near his right foot.

I knew he was telling the truth because I remembered that the floor around him was clear of any items. I looked at the pictures that Chris handed me and saw that they were pictures of Mrs. Jaeger, labeled 1959.

"Well, I guess she's telling us that she doesn't want me to go through her clothes. Sorry, but there are people who could really use your clothing," I said into thin air.

We went back to folding clothes and suddenly I felt something hit my ankle. I looked down and saw a small tan spool of sewing thread near my foot.

"That must have come out of one of the jacket pockets," I said to Bob, who just looked at me and patiently held open a bag as I filled it up.

Smack!

"What ... was that?" I asked

"Sounds like something hit the back wall over there," Bob said.

I went over to the sump pump drain, and found a small spool of red sewing thread on top of the drain cover. "Look at this," I said, half-laughing. I began to walk towards Chris and Bob. Smack! This time a brown spool of thread landed right near me.

"Where are they coming from?" I asked, not really thinking I was going to get an answer. Bang! This time it was a spool of black thread.

I spied a small turquoise velvet box on one of the shelves and remembered that it was filled with small spools of thread like the kind you'd get in a traveling sewing kit. I opened it and all the spools of thread were gone.

"I'll be damned," I said.

Then a music cassette tape hit the wall.

"Oh, no, here we go again," Chris said, "more poltergeist activity!"

Just then, the service man came down the steps and asked where the fuse box was, so I showed it to him.

"I can't understand," he said. "I checked the air conditioning before and it was working. Now I can't get any power."

He checked the fuse box and told me he was going to check the outside cable to the air conditioning unit to see if there was a short. As he went upstairs, Chris and I started to question whether some paranormal force was draining the power. We'd been trying to learn more about the paranormal to explain what we were experiencing, and learned the belief is that spirits will pull from the energy around them to manifest their power.

Bob disagreed. "There is probably a very simple explanation for the power loss," he said. He was still skeptical about what he was witnessing.

The repairman made more trips from the basement to upstairs, each time shaking his head as he failed to find the source of the problem. This went on for several hours. He would go upstairs and immediately something else was thrown. It got very funny and Chris was in hysterics. His laughter was infectious. Bob and I couldn't help ourselves. Something or someone was having a grand old time with us!

The items thrown were random and seemingly endless—a wooden Christmas ornament, travel slides, film cartridge and music cassettes hit the floor helter-skelter. I started a small pile on a shelf as I picked them up. As I made my way over to the wardrobe again, a dried rose hit my leg.

"How romantic," Chris said sarcastically.

"Give me a break," I said.

Suddenly Chris started to choke and spit something out of his mouth. He grabbed at it and saw it was a slender gold thread. He pulled it out of his mouth and found that the thread connected to a spool of gold sewing thread on the floor that still had sewing needles stuck in it.

"What the hell!" Chris said. "I can't believe this."

I looked at Bob, who now was speechless.

More stuff was thrown and then a red ball of knitting yarn with knitting needles stuck in it with a small knitted piece of an unfinished scarf seemed to appear out of nowhere on the small wine rack near the steps.

"I guess someone is trying to tell us something," Chris said. "Like get the hell away from *my* stuff."

He had just finished speaking when we heard a quieter smacking sound on the concrete floor on the right side of the steps. I walked over and laughed when I saw the same pile of black and white photos of Mrs. Jaeger that had begun the activity. After Chris had shown them to me, I watched him put them in a shoebox. Now, they were on the floor twenty-five feet away from that. Was Mrs. Jaeger telling us to get away from her things? Was the purpose of all this to delay us from removing her clothing? If that was her motive, she was doing a good job.

Bob started up the stairs with some of the twenty bags we had collected. I was following him when we saw a box of tissues being thrown to the ground along with a joke book, *Donkeys Don't Sleep in Bathtubs*.

Bob started laughing. "I didn't know that ghosts had a sense of humor." He continued up the stairs with the bags.

Chris came to see the joke book and we saw another book sail through the air and hit one of the wardrobes.

"Sly devils," I said. "Always one step ahead of us."

"I'm all done Ma'am. Would you sign the work order release?"

The repairman had come downstairs and was ready to leave. I found a cleared spot on the clothes dryer and signed the paper.

"You know this job should have only taken an hour, instead it took me three," the repairman said. "Everything seemed to go wrong. I don't understand why the power wasn't working down here."

"Umm...we seem to be having a problem in the basement and it may be affecting some of the power," I said nonchalantly. "Maybe you heard something?"

I didn't know what else to say to him. If he had seen or heard any poltergeist activity, he wasn't volunteering any information. Chris was looking at him and trying hard not to laugh.

"Is everything working now?" I asked.

"You're in good shape," he said.

Bob came down the steps and seconds after he did two cassette tapes flew by the man's head and hit the back wall. No one moved. The jig was up! The repairman's eyes grew wide as he turned to us.

"I heard THAT!" he exclaimed and then said something we'll never forget. "You people seem to have a MAJOR SPOOK PROBLEM down here!" With that, he took the signed paper and flew up the basement steps.

"Thank you," I called up after him. He didn't wait for me to show him the door. We couldn't stop laughing for the next ten minutes.

"And to think that my brother doesn't believe me about what's going on in the house," I said to Bob after we settled down.

He looked at me. "Really?" he asked.

"My mother mentioned something to him about the crazy stuff that's been happening and he doesn't believe it. I asked her not to say anything, but my mom can't keep anything to herself." I went back to looking through the clothes. "You didn't seem to believe what you saw here the last time either. How else do you explain what's been happening down here today if it isn't ghosts?"

Just as I said that Chris said, "Look Mom." He pointed to the top shelf of the wardrobe where Bob and I had been working.

"What is it?"

Bob helped me get up on a small stool and I grabbed what turned out to be a long roll of decorative wallpaper border.

"How did it get up there?" I asked. "It's really heavy and if it had hit either one of us it would have hurt."

I looked over to the shelf where I had made a pile from the objects I had picked up and the pile had disappeared!

"Anita, I'm going to call your brother and tell him about this." Bob said.

It looked like Bob had just become a believer.

—◊—

We worked for several more hours. What were we supposed to do? We had a job to do and the ghosts weren't about to stop me from what I planned to accomplish that day. More spools of thread rolled along the floor, slides were floating down everywhere, and it seemed as if the spirits were just being playful. They were also being annoying. I started to see fancy, vintage cotton hankies appearing and tossed lightly around the room, and that gave me the feeling that there was a decidedly feminine presence there. I'd found several hankies in the pockets of the clothes I was inspecting for donation, and put them on a counter near the wardrobe. They were in new condition with beautiful lace designs and I planned to rewash them and keep them for my doll costume projects. Nevertheless, they weren't the ones being thrown. Those seem to materialize from thin air.

Bob had to stop for the day and took the remaining bags upstairs for donation. We spoke briefly and I thanked him for his help. I saw him to the door and he kissed me and told me he'd call me to confirm plans for Saturday.

"Are you and Chris going to be ok?" he asked.

"We'll be fine. We're getting ready to call it a day too," I said.

He left and I went back downstairs and to where Chris was standing near the back row of wardrobes.

"Mom, can you help me get this movie projector out of here?"

"What are you doing with that piece of junk?" I asked him.

He motioned to the plastic wardrobes that were in his way. "Just hold these back," he said. He moved forward and in the light we could tell that the projector was rusty and in bad shape. I bent down to look at it.

"Crap, I thought we could use this at Kent's place," Chris said in frustration. As he started to stand up a pink cotton hankie fell on his arm.

"What the...?"

I stood up and a blue cotton hankie fell to the floor. I looked around. "Those two cotton hankies were over here," I said to Chris. I picked them up and put them back on the same table. "That was weird."

Chris turned around and a second later – swoosh - the blue hankie flew on top of the wardrobe and he began to laugh. "Look, Mom," he said and pointed it out to me.

"Do you have your cell phone? Get a picture!"

No sooner had he taken a picture of the blue hankie landing, the pink hankie quickly zoomed up right passed us and landed in the rafters in the ceiling. "Whoa!"

"Get some pictures of that!" I said.

Chris kept snapping away. "I don't know how good the pictures are going to come out," he said. "But at least we have a record of it."

"Other people may not believe us, but I know what I just saw," I said.

Ten minutes later, we started to pack the car and left the basement door open. I started down the basement steps for the last time.

"Chris, come here!" I said.

"What now?"

"Look." I pointed at the bottom of the steps and we saw a box of aluminum foil and a half empty bottle of WAWA iced tea that we had brought with us. We went down the steps and saw a painter's mixing stick propped up against the bottom step, yellow twist ties on another step, a blue milk bottle cap, large plastic trash ties and a pack of white post-it notes on the floor. All the items had come from the kitchen. We had never seen anything from upstairs thrown downstairs before.

"What's the point in all this?" I asked.

We picked the things up and went back up the stairs. Chris was walking ahead of me on his way out the door to throw some stuff in the trash. "Ouch," he said suddenly. "What just hit me?"

I picked up a small bottle of cologne off the floor that had been sitting on a shelf above the sink. "I think this just did."

Chris frowned. "Let's get out of here, please!"

"Ok, I've had enough too." I made my way over to the kitchen sink. "Just let me wash my hands."

Chris was closing the basement door when he suddenly freaked out. "I can't close it! It won't close all the way!"

"What?"

He looked terrified. "It feels like something is behind the door stopping it with their foot." He tried to put his full weight against it and the door still wouldn't close. Suddenly we heard a loud banging noise and the doorknob rattled in Chris' hand.

"Oh, Jesus Christ, I've had enough," Chris said as he jumped back from the door and ran out the kitchen door with me just behind him. A few seconds later, I looked back at the basement door and remembered that I had to close it or the alarm system wouldn't set.

"Don't go back there, Mom."

I mustered up my courage and went back into the kitchen. I stood in front of the door and said, "Please whoever you are let me close the door for security reasons."

Gingerly, I took the doorknob, was able to close the door quickly without any resistance, and bolted it at the top. My heart was racing. We drove home, emotionally drained.

Chapter 12

HAUNTED HOUSE?

Sometimes you can to be too close to a situation to be able to see how it is affecting you. You need to draw back, take a deep breath and look at it from a new perspective. After our strange experience on June 10, my son and I decided to call Linda, Jeff's legal assistant, and have her set up a meeting with the lawyer as soon as possible. Yes, Danny and Bob had seen the bizarre activity and so had the repairman, but in the cold light of reality away from the house we were scratching our head and questioning ourselves. *Did we really see that?* Was Paul or someone else really haunting the house?

We were now five months into working on the estate and things were getting weirder by the day. We wanted to know if this was going to continue for as long as we worked on the house, and what were our options? I felt that, in the rational world Paul's lawyer dealt with every day, he could possibly put this in a different light for us. In the end, he wasn't any help.

He was stunned, to say the least, when we told him about the experiences we were having at the house. He leaned back in his leather chair and shook his head.

"Yes, Linda mentioned something. I don't know what to say, Anita. This is very strange."

"But you believe us, don't you, Jeff?" I asked. "We think it was because we dug up the basement and disturbed things."

67

"We saw one TV show where these people bought an old house and were doing renovations when they started experiencing paranormal activity," Chris added, "That's similar to what we did."

"Look, I believe you, but this is out of my league."

"I wanted you to know and to have it on the record, Jeff. I didn't sign up for this."

"Well, what do you want to do?" Jeff asked. "You're in charge, but if for some reason you can't finish this I've been named as the next executor."

I knew he was right because I had read that clause in the will, too. With a busy law practice, the lawyer would never be able to do the kind of thorough job I was doing. I was certain that many valuable family heirlooms could be lost forever if I turned the job of executor over to someone else.

"I'm seeing this through to the end, Jeff," I said. "I have hundreds of hours invested in the estate, but if Chris and I start seeing coffins come up through the floor, we're out of there!"

Jeff laughed. "I think you guys need a break, take a few days off."

We agreed and as we left the office, my son turned to me. "We've only seen the lawyer once at the house and now he'll never come over."

Chris and I were making a point to watch the paranormal shows on TV, but as we watched the shows, we realized that they had nothing on us. We would watch and listen intently to see if they got a "hit" - saw a ghost on their thermal cameras - or heard an EVP (electronic voice phenomenon a.k.a. spirit voices) on their digital recorder.

My son and I laughed at the scant evidence they had caught during their hours of investigation and presented to their clients. We had experienced *hours* of phenomenon during our time in the basement compared to what little they showed. In addition, we still had months to go before we finished the job of cleaning out our "haunted house."

It's funny that we didn't call it that, we just said the house, but we had every right to call it haunted since we had all the criteria of one. We had residual haunting—something or any event played repeatedly, in a loop, without any connection to the surroundings. Those were the phantom phone calls from Paul's house. There was poltergeist activity - German for noisy ghosts - the countless items that were thrown in the basement and around us. Finally, intelligent haunting - the swift reply and interaction with the living from a spirit, like with Paul's communication. I was convinced he threw the religious medal when I asked him to give me a sign.

When I look back, I realize that during that time we were very innocent and unbiased. We were being open-minded and felt we were living through a truly unique situation. I was a trained artist and I used my heightened powers of observation to document the activity. Chris was also very observant and seemed very sensitive to the atmosphere of the house. We weren't reading any books about ghosts at the time since we didn't want the influence of a writer's point of view. We just wanted to observe, keep a record and remember in detail what we saw and heard. We knew we were involved in something extraordinary and it wasn't going away. Things seemed to be escalating and we felt we needed to document it on film and record any audio or visual evidence. Chris got out our old tape recorder and stocked up on tapes for his camcorder. We didn't want skeptics saying we were imagining this. We would be ready now if we witnessed any paranormal activity the next time we went to the house. Before we could do this, I had a meltdown.

II
HAUNTING DISCOVERIES

*"Words have no power to impress the mind
without the exquisite horror of their reality."*
- Edgar Allen Poe

Chapter 13

THE MELTDOWN

I didn't see it coming. After my meeting with the lawyer, I had a busy weekend schedule. On Saturday, Carl came down with his daughter and son to pick up the boxes I had packed for him and his family and to take Paul's bedroom furniture. By now, we had become friendly because I had taken extreme care to pack up his family heirlooms, books, photos, textiles and all his artwork that he had given his parents through the years. The first time he saw what I had done for him, like packing the set of his mother's china left to me in the will and instead boxing it up for his daughter, his icy veneer thawed and tears filled his eyes.

"I don't know what to say. Thank you, Anita."

I almost started to cry too. "Carl, I'm so sorry about how things turned out. I'll do everything I can to find every single thing mentioned in Paul's will for you and your family. I don't want your mother's china. I have my own. Give it to your daughter. At least she will have something from her grandmother to pass on to her children." Then I handed something to him. "This is for your son." It was a German Iron Cross, from World War I, that I had found in the basement, in a pile of junk.

"Oh God!" Carl said with surprise. "This belonged to my great-grandfather."

"I know. I have to find the other two that are mentioned in the will, but I'll find them. Don't worry. I'll leave no stone unturned."

Carl hugged me.

I didn't mention anything to Carl about the strange occurrences in the house, and things went smoothly the rest of the time he was there with no interference from any unearthly presence. After Carl left that day, I realized that all was quiet whenever he came to the house. Perhaps that was because the two brothers had a strained relationship during the last years of Paul's life and now that he was dead he still didn't want to have anything to do with his brother.

That Monday, June 15, the spirits gave us a bit of a reprieve from their spirited behavior. We decided to clear out his mother's closet filled with dozens of nightgowns, hundreds of dresses, skirts, blouses, slippers, stockings, blankets, hats and shoes. The list was endless. As Chris held one bag open for me to put in the last few items it would hold, he said, "Mom, feel this." He was just about to close up the trash bag with a twist tie when a blast of ice-cold air came out of the bag.

"Wow, Chris." I couldn't believe it. There was rushing cold air coming out of the trash bag; it lasted for about twenty seconds and then dissipated.

"That's so bizarre," Chris said and quickly closed the bag.

Finishing with the closet, Chris went through a small cabinet and sorted the VHS tapes he found in it.

"Maybe Danny could use this?" Chris remarked as he emptied the small wood laminate cabinet. "It's in decent shape. Do you know if Carl wants it?"

"I don't think so. I asked him the last time he came down if he wanted any furniture from this room, but he didn't seem interested," I said.

"Well, let me move this out from the corner and I'll clean it up and see if Danny wants it. I know he was looking for something to put his TV on." Chris easily lifted the empty cabinet away from the wall and dragged it across the area carpet.

"What's this?" He asked as he bent down to pick something up. Chris held up a thin black leather booklet that was about the size of a passport with gold embossing on the cover. "Look, Mom, this was under the carpet that the cabinet was on. Is that a Nazi insignia on it?"

"Let me see?"

There was no mistaking the markings. On the well-worn dark cover were the spread wings of an eagle on top of a swastika, the symbol of the German Third Reich.

"Mom, was Mr. Jaeger a Nazi?"

I didn't know. Paul once mentioned his father had been in the Navy but never mentioned that he served during World War II, and I never asked. I sat on the bed and scrutinized the booklet. It was some sort of a military I.D. book. It had fewer than 15 pages total. Inside, on the left hand side, there was a small photo of a young Mr. Jaeger in uniform. On the other pages were ink stamps of dates and locations. I didn't speak or read German but I could make out that it held a list of his inoculations against diseases during his time in the service, which dated from 1941. It stated he was married and that he had a wife, Hilda, and a son. I knew Carl was ten years older than Paul so the year of 1943 given as his birth date made sense.

"I think he was trying to hide that he was a Nazi, Mom. Why do you think it was hidden under the carpet?"

"I'm going to show this to your grandfather," I said.

My father had also served in World War II, in the Army Air Corp. He had been a radioman in a ten-member crew on a B-24 Bomber. His Bombardment Group, stationed in Italy, made bombing raids over Germany and the oil depots in Romania. He might know and help us to identify what we found.

I put the booklet away and finished packing up ten large trash bags filled with clothes needing to be washed over the next few days.

"You have to be kidding, Mom," Chris said.

I looked up at him as I tied a trash bag together and started walking towards the door. "What?"

"All this work you're bringing home. Just throw it in the dumpster."

"Look Chris, there are a lot of people out there who are less fortunate than us and if I have to wash a few loads of laundry so I can donate them to those families I'm going to do it. I would never put this stuff in a landfill."

"Ok," Chris said. "But don't snap at me when your back starts hurting you."

I didn't snap at Chris, but I did snap at the phone company when I got home. They were supposed to change Paul's phone service two weeks earlier, but we were still having a problem with Verizon.

"This is my third phone call and we need this fixed. Like I told you before the man's deceased and I'm in charge of paying the bills that are being forwarded to my address. No, I'm not his sister. Look, this is going nowhere. I want to talk to your supervisor."

This went on for two hours until I finally slammed the phone down, still not satisfied. No sooner had I hung up the phone than my Dad called. Since his Parkinson's disease made his voice weak and his words were sometimes garbled, he could just about get out what he wanted to say.

"Anita, I've been trying to call you for an hour."

I knew something was terribly wrong. "What's happened, Dad?" I asked.

"Your mother fell, she's in the hospital."

I learned that she had gone outside to their back patio to water some plants and had tripped and fallen. My dad didn't even hear her call for help, no one did. Bleeding profusely, she finally made it to the house, and called out for my dad. He saw her face covered in blood and called 911.

"Oh, God, Dad, I'll be there in a few minutes."

I switched gears and sprang into action. I quickly washed and dressed and Chris and I hurried over to my parents' house, which looked like a bloody crime scene, and called the hospital's ER. They assured me; she was being taken care of and was waiting to see the doctor. That gave me some time to throw dinner together for us and make sure Dad had his medication for his Parkinson's. Chris stayed with my visibly upset father and I drove to the hospital.

The traffic was slow and I grew impatient. I slammed my fist against the steering wheel. "God damn it! God damn it!" I yelled inside the closed car. I had to let it out. I was getting angrier by the minute. What else was going to happen? I was already stretched emotionally so thin. I kept thinking to myself, *what if my mother was seriously hurt? Who was going to take care of her? You- of course. Who else?*

"God," I yelled again. How much more can I take? Give me a freaking break!"

By the time I got to the hospital, I had composed myself. Nothing could have prepared me for what I was about to see. My mother looked like someone had smashed her face with a brick. Both her eyes were almost swollen shut and bruised black and blue. I was horrified. She started to cry when she saw me.

"Anita, I can't believe I did such a stupid thing."

I hugged her, she felt so frail. "Don't cry, Mom," I said. She had a fractured nose and cheekbone.

"Why did I go out and water those stupid flowers?"

I know why, I thought to myself, *because you can't sit still for five minutes.* "Calm down, Mom, you're making things worse."

The blood was still gushing from her nose and wouldn't stop because of the Plavix she was taking for her heart, so they finally had to plug one side with packing, which was very painful to do. The plug had to stay in for four days. Her swollen legs blew up like balloons, but thankfully, nothing was broken. The doctors said she was one lucky person and that if she had broken her hip at her age, 86, it would have been a fatal injury.

"She's a tough cookie," I told the doctor.

After he left the room, I realized no one had called my brother so I dialed his cell phone. "You want me to come over?" Tony asked. He told me his son was in the middle of a guitar lesson.

"No," I sighed, "it's okay. I'm waiting for them to get her a room."

I felt annoyed that my brother seemed to be getting another free pass. Once again, it was I in the emergency room with my mother. Waiting and waiting. I had been in this position ten times now in the last year and a half. My parents always called me first, never my brother. When my mother heard the nurse say that she was staying overnight, she started to complain.

"I don't want to stay here, I want to go home."

I got off the phone and looked at her in disbelief. I tried to compose myself because the frustration and anger I was feeling was going to make me say something I would regret later.

"Mom, are you serious? You had a terrible fall, you've lost a lot of blood and you're weak. There is no way you can put any weight on those legs and get into the car. You are staying here at least overnight. That's it."

Just then, the nurse came in again and echoed what I had just said and then verified that the doctor wanted her to stay in the hospital at least overnight for further tests. My mother started to cry again. She's not a good patient, can be very demanding and hates staying in the hospital, but in this situation she had no choice.

The nurses finally took her upstairs to a private room and I left after being there for over four hours. My mother was worried about Dad and I assured her I was going back to their house to get him settled for the night. Chris would sleep over in the spare bedroom so he wouldn't be alone. I was exhausted.

It was raining when I walked out to the car and as I drove home all my reserve and stifled emotions came out like a flood. I started to cry hot angry tears. I had been running on empty for some time and decided I could feel sorry for myself. For many months, it had been go-go-go, do ten things at once, never a chance to catch my breath. Everything for everyone else—I was becoming the consummate caregiver. Beginning with my parent's chronic illnesses and declining health followed by my stagnant art business, Rose's mother's sudden death, then Paul's untimely death, the all-consuming responsibilities of being the executrix of his estate, the nasty conditions at his house with the endless hours of backbreaking cleanup, and finally dealing with all the supernatural nonsense that had been going on. It was all emotionally draining.

Now with my mother's accident and its repercussions, I would be taking care of three households! I couldn't even think any more. The line, *God doesn't give you more than you can bear,* came into the mind. Really? I had reached my limit, but did not see any let up. I felt like I was ready for a straitjacket in a padded cell.

Chapter 14

SPIRIT PIXELS

After almost five days in the hospital, my mom came home. My brother came over to do some chores, my sister-in-law sent over some delicious food and when I came down with bronchitis and Chris developed a sinus infection, the hospital provided some home nursing care.

"Stress," the doctor said after hearing what I had been through during the past five months.

"No kidding. You don't know the half of it," I said in what little voice I had left. I didn't go to the house for almost a week but Chris and his friends drove over several times to check on things.

"Take a break," the lawyer had said.

Some vacation. Instead of lounging in the sun by a pool somewhere with a tall cool drink, I was in bed with a fever, coughing and downing Robitussin. However, taking some time off to recuperate gave me a chance to review the one good photo Chris took of the hankie that flew up the basement rafters. It was only a cell phone photo, and it was dark, but the resolution wasn't bad. The picture showed the hankie wrapped around a thick electric cable in the ceiling. I loaded the photo from Chris' cell phone into my computer software program, Photoshop. I took one copy of the original photo and hit a level tool in the software program to see if it would lighten the picture, but it didn't make it any better. It showed a slightly pink fuzzy cloth hankie in half shadow against a black background of the wooden ceiling rafters.

I looked at the digital photo closely with my trained eyes and thought I saw a slight whitish smudge in the blackness on the upper right corner of the picture. *What is that?* I thought to myself. I decided to crop the picture around the whitish area, which would make the area larger so I could see if there were any details. As I zoomed in close, it looked vaguely like a face. I had almost missed it. I was puzzled. What would have caused this white smudgy face when the whole area around the hankie was dead black? Was it a reflection of Chris' cell phone flash? No. The wood beams were so old and dirty and they weren't refinished with any varnish, so there hadn't been a reflection. I was frustrated because it was difficult to see any more details.

Then, I had a hunch. I used the level tools again on the cropped picture even though I thought it would be a waste of time. I say this only because once you use levels on a photo as I already had on this photo, it will not change anything further. However, I was in for a shock. I hit the level tool and what happened next is something I've never seen before in thirty-four years of working with photos.

The photo completely changed into a riot of bright colors of pixel mosaics and images. The main color was a solid deep yellow green with overlapping repeating blocks of colors: deep blues, turquoise, reds, oranges, purples, pinks, browns and grays scattered in no order. The faint whitish smudge at the center of it all was now an illuminated face with its own light source. Light wasn't reflecting on it to form an image, it was the *light!* It was also partially absent of pixels. How could that be? What in the world was I seeing? I didn't recognize the face, but I could definitely make out eyes, nose, a chin and the top outline of a head in bluish white tones. Unlike a standard 35mm camera that records an image on light sensitive film, digital photography uses light sensitive sensors to capture the image focused by the lens and stores it in a digital file ready for processing. You set your digital camera to dpi, which are digital pixels per square inch.

The pattern of pixels evenly spaced throughout makes up a digital picture surface like your TV screen. The higher the resolution (like 350 dpi), by using a good digital camera, the better it produces a sharper photo and the less pixilated (or fragmented) the images appear when blown up. The lower digital resolutions (72 dpi) can make an image fuzzy and distorted when enlarged.

As I blew up the photo further, I could see hundreds more tiny colored square pixels that overlapped in multi-layers to create dimension. This was the dark photo of only a moment ago. I could still see the cotton hankie, but the darkness around the hankie had changed into a crazy quilt of color. These weren't dust spots either, as you could make out designs and patterns. I had no idea where the color was coming from.

Then, it became incredible. Some of the pixels were blocks of variations of a solid color while others in their squares had what looked like objects in them! The more I looked at the tiny pixel squares, the more I started making out what looked like an ancient Greek shaped vase, some architectural features like doorways and arches, vertical and horizontal crosses, all different colors and sizes. Some of the squares were very bright white and others had shadows in them.

When I showed the photo to my friend Rose, who is an award-winning photographer, she was as baffled as I was. She could also make out designs and see objects as we navigated around the image. "Doesn't that remind you of some Aztec or Mayan temple?" she asked looking at one particularly interesting pattern.

She had a theory. She pointed out that white light breaks up into a spectrum of color when passing through a prism, and wondered if somehow we digitally shot through some type of spectral prism in the blackness that produced the colorful effect. It was an interesting concept but it didn't explain the artifacts.

Could it be possible that the image we digitally captured was holding fragmented memories of tangible thoughts? Did we accidentally photograph the essence of a spirited intelligence? Or were we looking at another dimension?

Chapter 15

CAUGHT ON TAPE!

"Hello? Testing, testing. We are here at Paul Jaeger's house today, where my Mom is the executor of his estate. It is June 24, and we are going to record any paranormal activities that occur while we work today. Let's see what happens."

Chris got the camcorder in focus and panned over the house. "Here's the side porch and there's my friend Eddie. Say hi to the camera, Ed."

"Hey, how's it going? Nice shirt." Ed pointed out the retro *Ghostbusters* shirt my son was wearing and waved at the camera. Eddie had eagerly volunteered when we asked for his help and was ready to go. His curiosity got the best of him when Chris told him he would be cleaning out "the haunted house." Eddie 'Breadsticks', Chris' good friend, a chef at one of the local pizzerias, had often been our "go to" guy to grab a quick dinner on days when we spent long hours at the house. He made everything homemade and produced some great subs and sandwiches for us in the past few months. He wasn't very tall but had tremendous upper body strength and powerful muscled tattooed arms, as he worked out regularly at the gym.

"And here comes my Mom," Chris said

I walked into view, looked at the camcorder, and said, "I just set up the tape recorder and placed it on Paul's bed in his room to see if we get anything on tape while we work downstairs. We feel it's time to try and officially record anything unusual happening today, if possible, and we are glad to have a witness to observe who can give us an unbiased opinion." With that said, we all made our way down to the dank basement to what would prove to be an eventful day.

It was the first time Eddie saw the house and the basement and we proceeded to familiarize him with the layout of the room, told him about our months of clean up and explained what we had to do today. He observed silently and finally let out a loud whistle. "You did this all yourselves. I'm really impressed."

"Well, with your help today, Ed, we will be one more step to accomplishing the impossible," I said.

"What's that stuff on the floor?" he asked.

Random things lay on the floor. They had been thrown when we weren't there: a sock, countless travel slides and several cassette tapes and a small pair of scissors.

"The more we clean, the more *they* trash the place again," I said with a sigh.

"They...you mean ghosts, right?" Eddie asked.

"Yep," Chris said, and rested the camera on a shelf. "See that hankie over there." He pointed to the pink hankie at the far end of the basement in the rafters. Since we could only reach it by using a ladder, we had left it there.

"Well, if those ghosts show up they'll have to deal with the Italian Stallion," Eddie said and flexed his muscles. He was also an amateur boxer.

With his *Rocky*-style hat and Italian facial features, he did resemble Sylvester Stallone. We laughed and started to work, and for a little while it was quiet, but that didn't last long. A small red pencil sharpener was the first thing thrown, and then a videocassette crashed against the wall. It was the 1950's movie, *The Egyptian*, a favorite of Paul's. Chris quickly grabbed the camcorder off the shelf.

"You have to hold onto the camera, Chris," I said. You didn't get that on tape."

"I won't be much help with the cleanup if I have to hold the camera," Chris said.

"Don't worry about that for now. Eddie will help me and you keep the camera pointed in our direction." Suddenly I had chills; they started from my shoulder blades and ran down my arms. I could see the hair standing up and got goose bumps. "Something's here," I whispered.

It became eerily quiet. A few minutes went by and nothing happened. Eddie and I started to pack some clothing in bags. We needed Chris to help Ed carry one of the bags upstairs so he placed the camcorder on a chair, aiming it down the long stretch of the back wall at the sump pump. A few weeks earlier, there had been a wooden partition dividing the basement into two rooms, now only the studs were left and the space was completely open. To the right of the chair and camera sat the clothes dryer, still connected by a long electric cable, pushed out ten feet from the back wall so it wasn't resting on the newly cemented trench. We went back to work with the clothes and a few minutes later we heard a loud bang. A music cassette tape landed near the drain.

"I hope that's on tape," Chris said as he walked into the view of the camera.

Eddie looked surprised to hear the bang, then shrugged his shoulders, took some trash up the stairs and said he had to use the bathroom. Chris picked up the camera and pointed to where the cassette lay on the floor. Suddenly a black magic marker flew from behind him and hit the clothespin bag that was hanging from a rod.

"I caught that!" Chris said.

He continued to pan around the basement towards me and another black object flew through the air behind him and hit the workbench.

"Mom, what was that?"

I ran over to the workbench and looked. "I think it was this black plastic ring."

Eddie came down the steps. "What did I miss, bro?" he asked Chris.

We told him what has just happened. "I'll show you the tape later, Eddie," Chris said.

Eddie was disappointed about missing the latest poltergeist activity. We went back to work near the wardrobes and Chris stood up at the bottom of the steps, resting his elbow on the left banister and holding the camera steady with two hands. We were about twenty-five feet away from him and he tried to get us and as much of the basement as he could within his view and let the camera roll. Suddenly we heard a loud noise, like wood hitting against wood.

"Okay, the cane just moved," Chris said cautiously.

Just opposite him, to the right at the bottom of the stairs, was an old wooden wardrobe cabinet filled with coats. It had a raised molded lip around the top where an old slide projector and a Christmas manger were sitting. Hanging from the molding on the side of the cabinet facing Chris was a light colored wood cane with a rubber safety tip on the end. We figured it had belonged to either Paul's mother or father at one time. We'd seen it so many times when we came down the steps that we never gave it a second thought.

"What do you mean it just moved?" I asked.

"I'm standing here with you and Eddie in the camera frame and the cane just moved!"

Ed and I held our ground, frozen to the spot. Chris couldn't believe what he had seen. "The cane just jumped and moved! I hope I got it. Let me make sure that I have the two of you and the cane in sight and see if I capture anything else."

Just as he steadied his arms firmly on the banister, the cane moved again. This time it actually jumped up and down higher than before with such force that it knocked off a thermometer that had been hanging further down on the side of the cabinet.

Chris was laughing when we ran over to him. He quickly rewound the tape. "Look! There it is!" He was so excited because he had caught the cane moving both times on tape. There was no denying it and he was ecstatic. He hoped, but never thought he would capture anything on tape.

"Can you rewind and see if we caught anything else on tape?" I asked him.

He took a brief moment to rewind some of the tape, and then played back the part where the camera was resting on the chair. "What...the hell is that?" he asked.

Right before the music cassette hit the drain, we captured something else on tape. We huddled around the camera's screen and kept looking at it, breaking down second by second.

"There, see that on the side of the clothes dryer?' Chris asked.

The angle of the shiny metal side of the clothes dryer acted like a distorted mirror and we could make out Chris' reflection of his black t-shirt and bare arms as he put things in a trash bag. You could hear us in the back of the room having a conversation about packing up the clothes.

Suddenly a tall, grayish, shadowy figure appears reflected on the side of the dryer, its dark transparency layering over Chris' more solid figure. In a flash, we saw a right arm movement that corresponded with the cassette tape thrown down towards the sump pump drain. It was incredible. No matter how many times we played it back, it gave us the chills each time. It was unbelievable. We had caught a ghost on tape!

"You still want to continue working the rest of the day, Ed?" I asked.

"I'm good," he replied, after we reviewed the tape for the fifth time. "But there is some really freaky stuff going on."

The freaky stuff continued.

Ed was standing between Chris and me when something else sailed through the air. The dim light bulb in the back area of the basement cast a pool of light near us and the shadow of the object thrown reflected on Eddie's large bare muscular shoulders as it flew by.

"Wow, that really flew from a distance," Chris said, looking up from the camera, when the pen landed near us.

"You're right, man," Ed said. "It came from way in back of you."

Ed stopped, looked around and then walked over to me near one of the wardrobes. He asked me if anything else needed to be packed. When he turned to face me, a large silver tube hit Eddie on his hand and he turned to Chris

"You throw a marker at me, Dude?"

Chris was stunned. "I...didn't hit you. That wasn't me. I'm trying to steady the camera by holding it with both hands."

I walked over to Eddie who still thought Chris was playing with him and looked down at the floor. There it sat - a large black and silver magic marker.

"Congratulations, you're the first person they ever hit," I said. "I don't think they like you, Eddie.

I laughed and Eddie started to smile, catching my joke.

"I'm telling you, dude, I didn't hit you with the marker," Chris repeated.

Eddie believed Chris and said, "F-'n ghosts."

Chris also followed that remark with a few choice words of his own and I glared at them and folded my arms across my chest. They saw the look of displeasure on my face and they apologized for the foul language.

"Look guys, let's not be disrespectful. We don't know *what's* doing this, but let's not make it any worse, OK?"

I was worried that their crude remarks were being heard by God knows what and would draw retaliation with horrible consequences. I was at the furthest back wall of the basement where we found an artificial tree under a cover near the largest wooden wardrobe closet. Paul loved to decorate this Christmas tree each year with the collection of hand blown ornaments he bought from Germany. The tree was bare, never to be decorated again and that made me lonely for Paul. Soon it would be in the trash and forgotten.

I opened the closet and found about twenty men's shirts from Mexico, a Peruvian alpaca poncho, sweaters and dozens of women's skirts and blouses. "Oh, God, not more clothes!" I said with a groan. "Look guys, we can go drink margaritas in this." I said as I held up one of the colored Mexican embroidered shirts.

I pulled them out and felt something fall near me. Chris still had the camera rolling and was able to capture that and what followed on tape.

"What fell near you, Mom?"

"It's a slide," I said and picked it up from the floor and held it up to the light. It was a landscape faded with time that I didn't recognize. No sooner had I put it down that another slide came sailing over to me.

"Where did that come from?" I held this one up to the light. "It's got people in it." I said to the camera. Then I recognized them. "It's Paul as a little boy with his father. Are you trying to tell me it's you and your dad here with us today Paul?" I called out.

Another slide flew over Eddie and Chris' head. "Dude, you see *that?*" Eddie shouted, all excited. "You're standing right next to me and that came from the ceiling over our heads."

We heard what sounded like a stick being dropped, over on the other side of the basement and went to investigate. Were Paul and Mr. Jaeger answering my question?

"Must be rats," Eddie said and laughed.

"You know we haven't seen a single living thing in this basement since we started cleaning up, Eddie," I said. "Not a cockroach, spider web or a moth or a fly. No signs of mice or rats or their droppings either. Not even an ant."

"Maybe a raccoon," Eddie said.

"No, Ed," I smiled. "This place has been a dead zone for a long time. I think the air is too toxic."

Chris grinned devilishly. "Yeah, it's only fit for the dead."

"Then, what the hell are we doing down here?" Eddie asked.

"Sometimes I wonder about that myself," I answered back.

We were near the now empty bookcases, not far from the drain where the workers had moved the washer. "Ok, who's doing this?" Eddie asked. "Someone's going to get a knuckle sandwich."

Just as Eddie made a pretend gesture, as if he were going to slam one of the bookcases with his fists, we heard a loud boom come from inside the washer.

Eddie looked at Chris. "Did you hear that?"

"Dude, it's like it answered you."

"You didn't hit the washer with your foot, did you?" I asked Chris.

Chris shook his head, and then tried to kick the washer with his knee in an attempt to recreate the same sound. We had no luck. It was impossible to reproduce the same booming hollow sound from outside the washer because it had come from the inside the washer.

We made our way back to the other side of the basement and Chris saw that the box that had once held the magic markers was now empty. *Sure, all of them had been thrown around the basement.*

We tried to go back to work, but it was difficult, with more slides thrown at us constantly. I thought I had packed away most of the slides I found, but there always seemed to be more. I had no idea where they were coming from.

"What do you want from me?" I finally yelled, exasperated. "I'm sorry you're angry that I'm getting rid of your clothes, Mr. and Mrs. Jaeger, but you're dead. What am I supposed to do with all this junk? Damn it!"

I was convinced that I was not only talking to Paul's spirit, but his mother's and father's as well. I also realized that Chris had caught my tirade on tape. I didn't care. I was tired of all the nonsense and I was going to finish the job whether they liked it or not.

"Hey, Mom, wasn't that red knitting yarn over there on the shelf?" Chris asked.

"Why are you asking?"

"It's gone now," Chris said.

I walked over to where it had been sitting. "Not again," I said

This was becoming a joke. The red ball of yarn with its attached knitting needles traveled around the basement more than we did. It would disappear and then reappear in another place.

"It will turn up. It always does," I said. I wondered why anyone in the afterlife would need knitting needles.

Eddie started to act like a goof ball and pretended to pierce his nose with a hanger. Then he poked his head through one of the wardrobes. "They're attacking!" he yelled and picked up a silver paper hat and tried to put it on Chris' head.

"Hey, man, what are you, five?" Chris asked, laughing.

"Just want to lighten the mood, bro." Eddie laughed and put on a leprechaun mask. "Where's me pot of gold?"

"Yeah, I'd like some of that," I said. "We should be so lucky."

Chris held up a pair of woman's slippers, which made about three dozen pairs of shoes, boots and slippers we had come across that afternoon. Most smelled so terrible and were so moldy that they immediately went into the trash.

"Do you think we have enough shoes, guys?" Chris asked, pointing to the slippers.

"No, Chris, give me *your* shoes," Eddie said unable to stop laughing.

Later, this nonsensical statement would become a catch phrase for our sanity. Whenever something got us down or we were bone tired or frazzled by the unexplainable or just plain scared, we would say, *"Give me your shoes."* Immediately we would laugh and feel better.

I picked up the red yarn from inside a plastic bin and held it up. "Look what I found," I said. It had traveled about five feet from where it had been sitting. Then I placed it back on the shelf and just watched it for a moment. "Let's see you move it with me watching."

There were two loose sheets of paper near the yarn, which was resting on top of some books. They were copies of an article Paul had written about St. Patrick's Day years earlier. I leaned against some of the boxes and stared at the yarn. Chris and Ed were on the other side of the basement so what happened next didn't record on tape. The ends of the two sheets of paper began to move as if an unseen hand was pressing them down with its finger.

"Guys, look at this," I said.

By the time they got there, it had stopped and when I told them what had happened Ed reiterated that there was some very freaky stuff going on.

"Danny told me about this place, but you have to see it to believe it," Eddie said, shaking his head.

"I'm going to check on the tape recorder in Paul's room," I said. "Why don't you guys finish up down here and bring those bags upstairs so we can call it a day."

"Okay, Miss A, but first Chris needs to *"Give me his shoes!"* Eddie grabbed my son around the waist and tried to pick him up.

"You're both nuts," I said and headed up the stairs.

I walked into Paul's almost empty bedroom and retrieved the tape recorder that I had placed on his bed. Only a clothes hamper, an old typewriter covered with a towel, and a large portrait painting of Paul leaning against the wall were left in his room. His large closet was emptied earlier of its hundreds of boxes of collectibles. It was hard to believe it was the same room. I brought the recorder to the dining room table and rewound it and found about two hours of tape had recorded.

When I played it back, I could distinctly hear voices on the tape. Had I captured audible paranormal sounds? Then I realized they were our voices coming from the basement right below Paul's bedroom. There wasn't any insulation under the hardwood floor and the room didn't have wall-to-wall carpeting to muffle the sound. I was sure our voices had contaminated the recording until I heard something interesting. Over our excited voices, over the paranormal activity in the basement, you could simultaneously hear either a knocking or a banging sound. I played the tape back for Ed and Chris when they came upstairs.

"It's definitely timed to exactly when things happened in the basement," Chris said. "But how come we didn't hear those bangs above us?"

It was a question beyond any rational explanation.

"I don't know. What gets me is that the knocks are coming right from Paul's room," I said. I paused and looked around the room, and noticed the portable typewriter covered with an old orange towel that had been pushed aside on one of the window ledges. I realized we had never even looked closely at it, as it was just another obstacle we moved out of our way to clear Paul's room. This time, something was drawing me to the typewriter to take the towel off.

"Guys, you are not going to believe this. Look!"

Chris and Eddie walked up to view what was a sheet of typing paper still in the typewriter's roller. Several of the typewriter's keys were stuck up in the air and jammed together. The paper was blank except for two typed words -"the hell..."

"Dude, really?" exclaimed Chris.

We stared at the typewriter and couldn't believe what we saw. My friend *had* to be the one who had typed the words but I had no idea when or why. I wondered, was this the source of the paranormal activity?

Chapter 16

FIREWORKS ON THE ROOF TOPS

Chris had another crazy dream. It was July 2 and we had planned to spend it at the house so we could take the long holiday weekend off. I took one look at him when he came downstairs for breakfast and I knew something was up.

"Could you tell your friend to leave me alone when I'm sleeping?" He said his eyes at half-mast.

"What's the matter?" I asked

"Paul came to me last night in a dream and told me to tell you not to forget about the fireworks on the roof tops. What's that supposed to mean?

I turned to him from the stove where I was preparing breakfast. "I don't know." The Fourth of July had always been an important holiday to Paul. He had written about it and had been a park ranger at Independence Hall during the summer Philadelphia's Bicentennial.

"Well, it sounds like some silly crap to me."

"Maybe Paul was trying to tell you something important, Chris. When we get to the house we will look for something with fireworks on it."

"Yeah, great. Yankee Doodle-Do-Do. Maybe fireworks will burn down that stupid house. I don't know what games Paul is playing with me but I'm getting really tired of it," Chris said with frustration in his voice.

Chris and I decided to work alone at the house. It would give me a chance to go through the rooms without interruption and not have to worry about supervising volunteers.

The basement was well on its way to being cleared out - which had been no easy feat - but there were still some small pockets of clutter and boxes on the shelves to go through. I decided we would only spend an hour in the basement and spend the rest of the day upstairs. We had the Purple Heart Charity coming the next day, Friday, and we planned to give them forty boxes of items, the maximum you could donate at one time.

We made our way into the basement and Chris shook his head. "I was hoping some white wizard would have waived his magic staff and all the rest of this would be cleared out," he said.

"No such luck, Chris, Gandolf has better things to do. We'll have to do it the mortal way and get our hands dirty. Oh, man, look at this place!" I walked and saw slides around the room in clusters, all over the floor. Although there had been a few things left on the floor, I knew that Chris and I hadn't left it that way.

Chris surveyed the basement and saw a trail of slides leading to the sump pump drain. "Oh, for crying out loud, look at all of this. It's been trashed."

"I don't get it," I said. "What's this supposed to mean?"

We wanted to be done as soon as possible so we could be upstairs the rest of the day. "I'm in no mood to start sweeping the floor again. Just leave it for now."

Chris helped me pack some boxes of books that the library didn't want. When he picked up a large book from a shelf, some 8"x10" black and white photos fell out from between the pages.

"Hey Mom, look at these." He held up some pictures of Paul in a swimsuit and in a business suit. "What was he, a model or something?"

"Yes, he was," I answered.

Paul had a long history of modeling that started in college. Shortly before his death, he told me that he had posed for a photographer friend of his for some new portrait shots and did some modeling for an art class.

"He was in good shape for a guy his age," Chris said

"Best shape of his life and he dies of a heart attack. Go figure." I couldn't get over the irony of it all.

Just then, a cassette tape flew through the air and hit the wooden magazine rack near Mr. Jaeger's workbench.

"Is that you, Paul?" I called out. "Are your parents here too?" We hadn't brought the tape recorder because we planned to get the work done and leave. Now I regretted that we hadn't. There was an eerie silence.

Nothing happened.

"Ok, well we have to get back to work," I shouted to no one in particular. *This is nuts.* I thought.

Bang! A slide hit the metal cabinet. "I'm getting pretty tired of picking up after you," I said.

Bang! Something hit the cement floor opposite from us. "What is this? Do you become brats in the afterlife?" I felt like I was dealing with mischievous three-year-olds.

"Mom, look there's a metal shovel in the bucket over there." We walked over to the bucket and saw a long-handled garden shovel inside it. "How the hell did it get in there?" Chris asked.

I looked at him and grinned sarcastically. "Are you forgetting that we're in the frigging fourth dimension of the Twilight Zone?" I asked

"Right I forgot!"

"If you want to use your energy to lift something that heavy why don't you pick up after yourselves?" I called out. "This place is a mess." I was angry now. "Yeah, what do you care...you're dead."

We picked up a few boxes to take upstairs when suddenly we noticed something different by the staircase. Every single slide and object that had been lying on the floor was gone.

"Are you freaking kidding me?" Chris exclaimed.

"Oh my God, Chris. Look!" I pointed to the shelf near the staircase. The slides were now neatly stacked, one on top of the other, in three piles.

"No freaken' way," Chris said shaking his head.

We put the boxes down and looked around. Everything cleared off the floor towards the sump pump, too. It was astonishing!

"Thank you," I said to the invisible cleanup crew. "Now, why don't you clean up the other side too?"

"I think you're pushing it, Mom," Chris said as he made his way upstairs again.

"If they are all sooo powerful," I gestured around with my hands as I followed behind him, "they can clean up the rest of the mess they made."

A few minutes later we returned to the basement and were talking about what to finish bringing up, when we stopped in our tracks. Every single item that had covered the floor near the wardrobe closets was gone. I looked around and saw some of the objects on the Franklin stove—a blue hanger, a box of tissues and a Christmas ornament in the shape of a dove. On the short metal table near the closets, the slides were neatly stacked in piles. I couldn't believe what I was seeing and started to laugh. Chris pulled off his Phillies baseball cap and scratched his head.

"Ok, they really listened to you, Mom."

I was dumbfounded. They had heard me and did what I asked. "No one's ever going to believe this," I said.

We didn't want to press our luck with the basement spirits any further so we headed upstairs. The living room had become a holding depot for the boxes for the Purple Heart the next day and was a mess. We decided to tackle the hall closet that was crammed with coats, hats, jackets, handbags, umbrellas and several vacuum cleaners in all sorts of sizes and shapes.

"There's a lot of good usable clothing in here that we can donate," I said reaching for a trash bag.

Chris adjusted his dust mask, hat and rubber gloves. "I'm going in," he said jokingly.

I laughed, but it was no joke. For the next hour, he dug through hundreds of musty items that hadn't been used in years. What a job! He was tossing things to me through his legs, like a dog sifting through dirt in search of a bone until he finally reached the back of the closet.

Chris came up for air coughing and with his nose stuffed up. "Oh, my God, I can't do this anymore. I feel dizzy."

"That's good for now, Chris. Let's take a break," I said.

"Before you move Mom, let me give you some moldy *shoes*."

I wrinkled my nose in disgust and tossed them in the trash bin.

While eating a snack at the dining room table, Chris mentioned his dream again. He was looking into the living room at a small faux leather chest that was on the bottom shelf of a table near the picture window. He stopped chewing on his apple and said. "Did you check out that chest, Mom?"

"That? I looked at it once briefly and I think it's just a collection of music CD's."

Chris intrigued, walked over to the chest, and opened it. I had walked into the kitchen to put the ice tea back into the fridge and looked around for a magic marker to mark the boxes for the Purple Heart.

Suddenly Chris let out a happy yell and came running into the kitchen. "Look what I found." Chris had a CD in his hand. I looked at it and saw a picture of an American flag and a fireworks display over city buildings and rooftops on the cover. The CD featured patriotic music for the Fourth of July.

"Don't forget to tell your Mom, fireworks on rooftops," Paul had told Chris in his dream."

"Wow, that's crazy!" I said

"It gets better," Chris said with a big grin "Look what I found wedged in back of the CD. Chris held up a small piece of tissue paper and inside it was one of the long lost Iron Crosses that had belonged to Paul's great-grandfather. I had promised Carl I would find them all for him, but it hadn't been easy.

"Keep dreaming, kiddo. I think you are on to something. Maybe next time he'll tell you where to find the lost city of Atlantis," I laughed.

Chapter 17

NOW YOU SEE IT, NOW YOU DON'T

July 7th

"Hey Danny, hey Eddie, I'm glad you guys could give us a hand today," I said as they got out of Danny's car.

"Hey Miss A, did you have a nice Fourth?" Danny asked and gave me a big hug.

"It was nice. Do you guys want to stop at WAWA before we go to the house?"

My son and his friends looked at me with big smiles on their faces. "Oh, boy, chicken corn chowder," they said in unison.

—⁂—

"Let's finish cleaning this work bench and go through these side boxes here," I pointed out to Chris, Danny and Eddie as we worked in the basement.

Danny and I tackled the boxes and Chris and Eddie started clearing the top of the workbench. Eddie held up a plastic desk nameplate and asked me if I wanted to keep it. Before I could answer, a small picture of Paul in his workout clothes was flicked at us, like a Frisbee, and landed on top of the workbench.

"Hel-lo," Danny said, laughing. By now, he and the others were paranormal veterans. They were just curious to see what would happen next.

"Is that him?" Eddie asked and picked up the photo.

"Yes, that's Paul in his later years," I answered. "I don't think I'll throw out that nameplate just yet."

We continued working when a spool of thread flew across the room. "Here we go again," Danny said.

"Ok, let's try and finish here as soon as we can, guys," I said.

No sooner had the word come out of my mouth than a book on angels flew near us from the back wall of the basement.

"Is he trying to tell us something Miss A? Is he an angel?" Eddie asked me sincerely.

"I don't know," I said. "If it's Paul, I don't know why he'd still be so attached to all this earthly junk."

I turned back to the workbench and a packet of 3x5 index cards hit me squarely in the shoulder. "Ouch! Hey, that hurt!"

"Maybe he didn't like the fact that you insulted his stuff, Mom," Chris said.

"That's too damn bad," I shouted. "I'm sick of this bullshit!"

Danny gave me a sympathetic look and patted my arm, and I tried to calm down. Eddie took down a small, carved wooden sword from the top of an old freezer and pretended to fight with an imaginary enemy. The tense mood was broken when a National Geographic magazine hit the metal locker five feet away. It hit with such force that it made a large dent on the side of the cabinet.

"Jesus, did you see that? They mean business, dude," Eddie said and hurriedly put the sword down.

"Mom, let's take the things we've been through upstairs and concentrate there and in the garage. I think it's getting too dangerous for us to keep working down here today."

"Sounds like a plan, Chris," I said, grateful for having raised a sensible kid.

I was worried now that something more malevolent was down in the basement with us. I had never felt threatened before, but now I did. In the past, they had thrown things that were light, but today they had thrown something heavy and we could have been hurt. Within minutes my fears were confirmed, when we heard a loud bang. We froze. Chris was brave and went over to investigate. On the concrete floor, he found a large two-inch metal screw bolt with a square washer still attached to it.

"Look at the dent it made on the metal cabinet." Chris yelled. "This could have killed someone if they had been in its path!"

Eddie and Danny were too afraid to move.

I started to panic. I was responsible for their safety while they were in the house. I was sweating hard and could now feel the perspiration pour down my face. I didn't want to push our luck. The atmosphere was turning dark and menacing. I sensed we could be in real danger. "Ok, you made your point!" I yelled to the spirits. "We're going!"

—⚏—

The right side of the garage had been clean for over a month. Paul's car was left to his brother, so Carl and his son had picked it up weeks ago. The empty side gave us a clear area to sort and pack up items. We worked in two teams again. Danny and Chris were sweeping up the debris that hadn't been touched in years and were putting it in the trash. Eddie stuffed the recycling bins with endless bundles of newspapers we found and took them out to the curb. I sorted through more books and secured the boxes for the Purple Heart. For several hours, we were very busy and managed to get a lot of work done.

"Mom, come here."

I didn't like the way that sounded.

"What Chris?"

"Look. I just got hit with this as I came out the kitchen door." He pointed to a yellow plastic hanger that was lying in the driveway.

I picked up the hanger and a red sponge that I used in the kitchen sink flew out the door behind Chris. "Whoa!" I said. "Those things followed us out the door."

"Hey Miss A, do you want us to start piling the boxes and bags in front of the garage door?" Eddie yelled.

"Don't say anything to the guys, Chris, but let's finish up and get out of here," I said quietly, Then, I turned around, "Yes, Ed, go ahead and do that and I'll grab some bottles of water for you and Danny."

I made my way into the kitchen to get the water and saw that a box of blue-striped soda straws were tossed around the floor like pick-up sticks.

"Oh, for God's sake," I said.

Chris heard me and poked his head in the door.

"This is crazy," I said. "I think these bratty ghosts need a time out."

It was the end of a long day for us. Neatly piled in front of the garage and tagged for pick-up were forty boxes and bags. I went out to the porch and pushed the button on the remote, pointed it at the right garage door and closed it. I made a final sweep of the place, shut off the lights and made my way over to the kitchen door. The boys were outside talking and waiting for me to take them home. When I walked over to the door ready to set the alarm, Chris called out to me, "Did you forget something in the garage, Mom?"

"No. Why?"

"The garage door just went up."

I was puzzled. "Wait, maybe I didn't press the button hard enough." I picked up the remote that was on the kitchen table, walked out onto the porch, and aimed the remote in the direction of the garage. I pressed the button again and the garage door closed.

"Ok now?" I asked, as I headed through the kitchen door.

The boys started to laugh again.

"No, the garage door just went up again." Chris answered.

"What the hell?" I walked out and over to the garage door. "Chris, go inside and press the remote button when I tell you and I'll check the sensor light. Maybe there's something obstructing the beam." I bent down and cleaned the light sensors of any dirt or cobwebs I saw. "Press it now."

The door came down again and I guided it with my hand until it met the ground firmly. "That must have been it."

Chris was outside by now and when I turned my back and began to walk away the door started going up again. The boys were howling!

"What's going on?" I asked. "Chris, where's the remote?"

"I left it on the kitchen table."

"Go get it because there's something strange going on."

Chris and Danny ran inside only to run back out a few seconds later. "It's gone!" They said in unison.

"What do you mean it's gone?" I asked.

"I left it on the kitchen table and it's not there. How could it have disappeared?"

This was getting too weird for me. What was I going to do? I couldn't leave the garage door open since we'd already had one attempted break-in. The other garage door's remote system was broken and we had to lock that door from the inside by wedging a wrench into the track. We only got in and out of the right door using the remote. It was getting late and we had to leave soon because Eddie had to be at work for the dinner rush. Our experience with objects disappearing and reappearing at the whim of the spirits wasn't a good one. I didn't need this now and couldn't decide what to do.

"Guys, look around for the remote."

While they looked around everywhere I got angrier knowing the search would be futile.

"What are we going to do, Mom? It's not here."

I thought for a moment and decided enough was enough. "I'll tell you what I'm going to do. I'm going down to the basement and give those SOB ghosts a piece of my mind!"

The boys had never seen me so furious. I was tired and dirty and fed up with the paranormal nonsense.

"Go Mom!"

I walked into the house and marched down the basement steps with purpose. *I'll show you who you're dealing with,* I thought. I was too angry to be afraid. When I got to the bottom step, I yelled, "Ok, whoever you are, listen up! The remote is missing and I know you think it's funny, but it isn't. If you don't give me back the damn remote, I'll bulldoze this f**king house down, so help me God!"

That moment of silence felt like an eternity until Chris and Danny yelled out, "It's back, the remote is back!"

"That's more like it," I said to the invisible pranksters.

I walked back upstairs, relieved that the remote was back. We closed the garage door again and this time it stayed closed. I put the remote in my handbag and never again left it on the kitchen table.

—⁂—

There was a thunderstorm later that night and I was glad I'd put a large plastic tarpaulin over the cardboard boxes for the Purple Heart. At home, I asked Chris to hang a few delicate blouses on the shower curtain rod in the downstairs bathroom off my studio. I had just washed our sweaty work clothes and put them in the dryer. Chris walked into the kitchen and asked if dinner was ready and we both heard a familiar thump. We looked at each other, afraid to say what we were both thinking. Chris spoke first.

"What just got thrown?" he asked.

We went into my art studio and found a box of leather driving gloves on the hardwood floor.

"Where did these come from?" Chris asked.

I had a sinking feeling in my stomach, as I knew exactly where they were from. The gloves and several boxes of old postcards and new greeting cards were being stored in our downstairs bathtub. My studio had become crammed with boxes of Paul's writing materials and since we never used this bathtub, one day out of desperation, I dumped the boxes there and closed the shower curtain. No one could tell the boxes were there unless they pushed back the shower curtain, which Chris did to hang up the blouses.

"Are they Mrs. Jaeger's gloves?" my son asked.

"They were in her drawer along with a dozen other pairs," I answered.

"That's just great," Chris said. "Looks like someone came along with the gloves."

"But...I only kept a couple of pairs," I said apologetically. "Do you really think something came home with us?"

We went back into the kitchen. By now the thunder and lightning was constant and the rain pelted against the windows. As Chris walked by the kitchen doorway, a brass doorstop that was leaning against the dining room wall topped over.

"I think I must have done that, Mom."

I was skeptical. The door stop had been there for months and never once fell over no matter how many times we walked by it. Suddenly, we heard two smacks coming from my studio again and ran back in. We saw nothing. I decided to investigate further, and went into the bathroom and found two glove boxes on the tile floor. How could it be possible that they had jumped out of the tub?

Still not sure what was going on, we went back into the kitchen where I had been at the sink mixing a container of ice tea. Suddenly, I jumped back and watched as the white lid to the container flew from the sink through the dining room and landed in the living room.

"What's going on?" Chris asked.

A bolt of lightning flashed through the windows as I ran into the living room feeling as if I was in some kind of cheesy horror movie.

"OH NO YOU DON'T!" I was furious and shouted again. "Don't you dare start throwing things in my house. Get the hell out of here right now and go back to that black hole you call home!" I tried to catch my breath as I finished my warning. Had some ghost attached itself to me from the house? Was that even possible? Things abruptly stopped, but for how long?

Chapter 18

INCIDENT IN THE GARDEN HOUSE

"Look out Mom!" my son yelled.

He swiftly put up his hand to protect the right side of my face and at the same time batted down something that had flown through the air from behind us.

"What just happened?" I asked him in astonishment.

He pointed to a music cassette tape that was now lying inside the bottom of a cabinet. His quick reflexes had enabled him to smack the cassette in mid-air so fast that the tape bounced into the cabinet.

"That tape flew right for your head!" my son explained.

Shaken, I looked at the tape now lying just inside the open door of the cabinet. "Thanks. My God, where did it come from?"

He turned around and pointed to a stack of music tapes in the far right end corner next to the door. "That would have really hurt if that had hit you in the face," he said.

"You're right. It's a good thing you were standing next to me." I said.

It was a warm day in July and we had been inside the "garden house" for about an hour, trying to sort through the stacked boxes and bins of junk that filled it to the top of the ceiling. In the last few days, we had gone through the first 10 boxes that were stacked in front of the door. We finally made our way to the end of the 12 x 16 foot long masonry structure that Paul's father had used for a carpentry shop and potting shed. Afterwards, Paul used it as a catch-all to store all kinds of junk. His father had built the cabinets on the bottom for storage, with a level counter top for tools and planters, and then side cabinets, drawers and shelves to hold various outdoor gardening and power tools.

We had removed the magazines from the bottom cabinet and placed them in boxes out on the lawn so we could have room to sort through items and decide what to throw out, what to donate and what to keep. I had been in the shed by myself for about a half hour when I thought I had heard something drop on the counter top I was clearing. I looked at the accumulated junk, pots, papers, tools and magazines I was stacking on the counter top and noticed a square tan beer coaster that hadn't been there a minute ago. I shrugged it off and then a plastic ID card dropped on the counter, too. I picked it up, turned it over, and saw it was a photo ID badge of my friend when he worked at a local department store. My son had just come into the shed and I told him about the thrown badge and then showed it to him.

"You sure you didn't just dislodge it from a pile that was over here?" he asked.

"I don't know. There's so much on top here. We never had anything thrown outside on the grounds this far from the house and never in here," I said.

We continued looking through a huge box of newspapers and what-nots, and both thought we heard something else drop behind us. I was now more concerned that the activity we were experiencing in the house could be following us. First, it was at my house in my studio and now here, outside of Paul's house. I had pretty much been spared being hit with objects, but Chris, his friends and my friend, Bob had all been hit on more than one occasion. *It or they* seemed no longer confined to just one place. How was this happening? Had we somehow unleashed a ghostly energy and they were spreading their presence like a virus around and now getting stronger. I didn't like it and was more angry than scared. There didn't seem to be safe place for us on the property. The thought was unsettling as we still had several months more of work to do to clear out the house for sale. So many people including Paul's brother and family were to get specific items mentioned in his will and we still had to find some of them. Quitting crossed my mind several times but I felt I had to keep my promise. There was no turning back now.

Bob, who had joined us today, poked his head inside the shed and asked what other bags had to go out to the trash. We looked around to see what work we could save for another time and decided to call it quits for the afternoon. It was getting very hot in the shed. Chris stepped outside and busied himself tying up another black trash bag. I was talking to Bob when I walked out the door, being careful to watch where I put my feet, as there were boxes on either side of the brick walkway. All of a sudden, I felt pushed from behind and fell to the ground. It happened so fast and I was so taken by surprise, I couldn't catch myself. I landed on my right knee and my left leg hit boxes. I fell over several others and that broke my fall.

"What just happened, Mom?"

My son looked incredulous. He had been sitting on the ground putting things in a trash bag and Bob was looking down at him waiting for him to tie it up so he could take it out to the curb. They both couldn't catch me, it happened so suddenly.

Bob lifted me up from the ground and seemed just as surprised as I was. "You ok?" he asked.

"Dammit, I don't know!" I yelled. "I just got pushed! I am so out of here," I said as I rubbed my thigh. I would develop a large nasty purple bruise on my left thigh that would last for over 2 weeks.

Before we left, I went in to retrieve the mini tape recorder I had set up in the basement. I had left it on record while we were outside. I was hoping we had picked something up on the tape. I would have to review it later that evening.

That night we listened to the 45-minute tape and caught some interesting noises. In the background was the sound of us as we went in and out the kitchen door. There were several sections on the tape with loud bangs and sounds of movement in the heart of the basement without anyone being present. One particular noise sounded like a person saying in a whisper, *"Help!"*

It sounded like a man's voice. Why was he asking for help?

There was a long sequence of loud bangs, things being thrown and something metallic being scraped and dragged across the bare concrete floor. It sounded creepy and it made my blood run cold.

Little did we know, *the worst* was yet to come.

Chapter 19

THE APPARITION

July 21st

After the pushing incident, we were able to work in peace for a week and a half. Perhaps the ghosts had exhausted their energy with all the paranormal activity they had inflicted on us and had made their point in hurting me. Now it seemed they planned to make up for lost time.

Once again, Danny was able to help us out for the day. No sooner had we walked into the kitchen, Danny and I heard a woman's voice call out from the basement. *"Who's there?"*

Chris was still outside on the porch and didn't hear the voice.

"What's going on?" he asked as he walked into the kitchen.

"Danny and I just heard a cough and then a woman's voice calling out to us from the basement."

"Are you serious?" It was the first time we had *heard* a voice that wasn't on tape.

"We're not going to work in the basement today, are we?" Danny asked anxiously.

"No, I'm just going to set up a tape recorder down there and retrieve it later. Let's concentrate on the "cat room" today and clear that out," I said.

For the next several hours we worked in the cat room - or spare room - and emptied its contents—magazines, papers and reference materials. Danny made several trips to the porch and the recycling bins and each time he came back into the spare room he remarked that he heard noises coming from the basement and scratching noises coming from behind the walls. Chris also acknowledged that he heard the same scratching noises.

"Do you think that sounds like an animal?" I asked them. "Maybe it's a cat?"

"That's a good description," Danny said. "Did the guy have cats?"

"When he died he had two of them and he also had a cat named Heidi that died 3 years ago. He loved cats and so did his mom," I said.

"Can cats be ghosts?" Chris asked.

"Anything's possible, I guess. Maybe they're all here," I said.

Chris laughed. "Well, why not? The more the merrier."

We made our way around the small room and removed the boxes piled in front of the closet. I opened the closet and found it jammed with women's clothes—coats, jackets and dresses.

"Jesus, does it ever end?" I asked in frustration. "How much did one person need?"

We stripped the dusty and hairy covers off the day bed and put them in a trash bag. The bed was down to its bare mattress and I now had a clear surface to use for sorting and packing. Chris swept the room and the hallway rug and I started to go through the closet. There were department store boxes stacked on the top shelf and containers of sewing supplies on the closet floor. I found an old hair dryer and shoe boxes filled with old photos that I put aside for Paul's brother. I took out the department store boxes that held dress patterns, swatches of vintage material, personalized dress labels, and put them on the bed. Mrs. Jaeger had been an expert tailor and I planned to give these things to her granddaughter, along with the sewing machine I found in the room. When I emptied the shelf, I found a small cardboard box and brought it out for a closer look.

"Oh, my God, it's Heidi!" I yelled. Chris and Danny ran into the room.

"What's wrong?" they asked.

I showed them the plastic sealed box from a local pet cemetery and crematorium that held the cat's ashes. There was a small-inscribed plaque on top of the box with the words: *"Heidi Jaeger, Beloved Pet"*- *Oct 13, 2006*

"Are you serious?" Chris asked.

I handed him the box. "Look for yourself."

"There's no way I'm touching that." Chris recoiled from me. "Why in the hell didn't he bury the cat?"

"I don't now, but if I had found this sooner I'd have given it to the lawyer and had him scatter Heidi's ashes with Paul's out in Colorado. Now, what am I supposed to do with it?"

"Well, I think you know where I'd like to shove it," Chris said.

Danny snickered as I looked at the cat's box in my hand.

Yet another piece of Paul's unfinished business I'm going to have to deal with, I thought.

"Well at least now we know why we've been hearing scratching noises for the last half hour," Chris said. "I bet it's the cat."

He walked out of the room and when he passed by the full-length mirror in the hall he let out a yell. "The mirror just fell over!"

We went on full alert.

"Danny and I have trash to put out so we're going outside. I've seen enough weird shit for the moment," Chris said

I walked over to the bed. "Before you do, take some of these boxes and stack them in the corner of the living room with Carl's other stuff. Thanks."

They left and I returned to the bed and began to sort clothes from the closet. I had my back turned to the doorway when suddenly I heard a plop! I looked down and saw a packet of German brand facial tissues lying on the floor that I remembered seeing in the kitchen. No sooner had I picked them up than I heard another bang and saw an old-fashioned men's shaving brush on the floor.

"Hel-lo? Guys?"

I walked into the hallway and no one was there so I knew the boys were still outside. I went back into the room and a spool of blue sewing thread and a brown converter plug hit the door. From where I stood, it looked as though they had come from the direction of the dining room.

"Nice shot," I called out. Then, I ran out of the room and went to get Chris and Danny.

"There's stuff being thrown in the cat room, guys," I said

They came running into the kitchen. "What's going on?" Danny asked.

Chris sat down on a kitchen chair and Danny stood near the open basement door while I explained to them what had just happened

"Something's upset that we're cleaning out the cat room," I said.

Chris was disgusted. "That's just too damn bad they're upset. We've been at this for six months and still have a mess to clean up before we sell this crappy place," he said.

"I know. I'm waiting for that one real estate agent to get back to me with a possible offer. If it's reasonable, I'm taking it."

"Well nothing is getting done with us just standing here," Chris said. "Come on Danny, let's get back to work."

Danny did not answer us.

We both turned to where Danny had been standing the whole time near the open basement door.

"Whatayoudoin, Danny?" Chris asked. "Are you having a brain fart?"

He stood frozen to the spot. I had never seen Danny look so frightened. He tried to speak but could hardly form a coherent sentence.

"I…just…saw…a…guy walking around…at the bottom of the steps and it scared the hell out of me!"

"What?" Chris and I said at the same time.

Danny swallowed hard. "I just saw a man…with dark hair, beige pants, brown shoes and a light colored shirt, walk across the bottom of the steps."

I quickly walked over to him.

"See, he's right there." Danny pointed into the dark basement.

I could hardly believe what he was saying. Had Danny just seen a ghost and a full body one at that? I was almost too afraid to look. I peered down at the bottom step and saw nothing.

"Look, now there's a shadow near the freezer,' Danny said.

I still wasn't sure if I saw it too. Something seemed to dash to our right as we turned the lights on and Chris and I went slowly down the steps and looked around the basement. Everything seemed quiet, a little too quiet. The tape recorder was still sitting on the table where I had placed it several hours earlier. Seeing that it was finished I picked it up and took it with me, thinking that I would listen to it later. As Chris and I headed upstairs, a packet of slides and two cassette tapes crashed to the floor towards our direction. We flew up the steps and closed the basement door.

Danny still looked pale and shaken when I questioned him.

"Was the man tall or short?" I asked.

"He was tall," Danny said empathically. "I still can't believe what I saw."

"Sounds like my friend Paul," I said, but of course I couldn't be sure.

Danny was still mumbling about the apparition when Chris put his hand on his shoulder. "I think we should take a break for lunch. Ok, Danny?"

"Huh? Ok."

He perked up when I said I had brought chicken corn chowder.

—〰—

"Oh my God!" I screamed. "What happened? What got thrown now?"

We had just finished a late lunch. Chris and Danny were getting some trash from the back room when the next wave of paranormal activity occurred. There was a sickening loud crash.

"What just fell? Are you guys all right?"

I heard Chris and Danny yelling.

"The room divider fell over on the wall next to us!" Chris yelled from the back hall.

I had just put a new tape into the recorder when Chris ran into the dining room.

"It came crashing down next to us when we walked by the mirror," Chris said.

"Oh my God, if that had hit you guys..." my voice trailed off.

The tri-fold room divider was solid wood and weighed at least fifty pounds. We never had much paranormal activity upstairs before this, but the fact that we were cleaning out the cat room had made someone angry and the activity had escalated.

"There's so much stuff going on today it's ridiculous," I said. "We have to get some pictures."

"I didn't bring my camera," Chris said as Danny walked into the room.

"Wonderful," I said. "It would have been a great day to get pictures of all this."

"Holy shit!" Danny exclaimed.

The plastic covering for one of the heating vents had flown into the living room missing Danny's head by only a few inches.

Chris immediately grabbed a plastic bat and Danny grabbed a wooden dowel stick.

"They're already dead! You can't hurt them," I said.

"I feel better with something in my hands," Chris said. "At least I can block whatever comes my way."

"Do you hear scratching noise?" Chris asked.

"It's the God damn cat," Danny retorted.

We listened closely to the scratches coming from behind the walls.

"GEEEETTTT OUUUTTTT!"

Terrified by the unearthly voice that came out of nowhere, Chris, Danny and I ran into the kitchen, but Danny said the scratching noises were following him.

"What the frigging hell was that?" Chris asked.

"I think they want us out of here—yesterday," Danny said.

"Who? The cat? Or, the whole family?" Chris asked.

"The hair just stood up on the back of my neck," Danny said. "This is seriously weird."

"Maybe we should leave for the day," I said. "I mean this stuff is just going to keep happening."

Danny didn't seem to hear me.

"Is the water running?" Danny asked suddenly.

"I don't think so," Chris said.

Danny stayed in the kitchen while Chris and I went to check the bathroom to see if the water was running. It was not. What was Danny seeing and hearing that we were not?

"Hey, why don't you love me?" We heard Danny's voice from the kitchen. He seemed far off in the distance

"I wish he would be quiet. What's he doing, anyway?" I asked.

"I think he's singing," Chris said

"Tell him to keep his day job."

A loud bang and some other strange noises followed.

"Did you hear that?" I asked. "It sounded like a wind-up toy or something musical."

"No," Chris said. "Maybe Danny started something by singing. Who knows? That bang was really loud, though."

"I know," I said. "Let's go check on Danny."

We went back into the kitchen and asked Danny if he'd heard anything sounding like music. He said he hadn't, but that he still kept hearing scratching noises all around. While we stood in the kitchen, a black magic marker flew out of a cup holder on the kitchen table and landed in the sink. We all laughed.

Danny suddenly noticed a spot of blood on Chris' shorts. "Hey man, did you scratch yourself? Look."

"No. Where did this come from?" Chris said looking up at the ceiling and around the kitchen.

Chris pulled up his shorts to see if there was a cut on his leg and saw nothing.

We all retraced our steps, and walked back to the living room to look around for other signs of blood spots and suddenly I grabbed Chris' arm.

"Look at that!" I pointed to the statue of the Veiled Lady.

We now saw a drop of blood running down the cheek on the statue's face. I started to feel cold chills down my spine. We all froze in our tracks.

"Dude!" was all that Danny could say.

I was the first to move and got a cold wet washcloth from the kitchen to help Chris wipe the blood from his shorts. Looking down Chris noticed the blood was gone! Still shaking our heads we looked at the statue, the blood was gone there, too. Were we all hallucinating? Any proof of the blood had just evaporated.

"Look! Do you see that?" Danny asked, pointing across the room. He was crying and laughing at the same time.

"Oh Jesus Christ!" Chris yelled and jumped back. "A black shadow just went by on the wall."

"That's it! I've had enough. Let's call it a day, guys," I said and quickly went back to the cat room and picked up some bags of clothes to take out to the car. "I have no idea how we're going to get anything else done today," I called back to Chris.

There were still piles of clothes on the bed.

I'll get the rest of these clothes another day, I said out loud to myself.

I heard an unearthly voice say *"YESSSS!"*

"Ok, ok, I'm going," I said to the entity in the room.

"Ouch! You son of a bitch!" Danny yelled suddenly.

I ran back into the living room.

"What happened?" I asked.

"Danny just got hit with a roll of duct tape and I got hit with several paper clips," Chris said.

"Let's stay together," I said. "Leave the trash alone for now and help me get these bags together to bring to the car."

Everything was fine for a few minutes. Then the silence was broken when we began to be pelted with books and pens. One book ricocheted against the ceiling and bounced back to the floor.

"Whoa," I screamed "Everyone, move!"

Things flew around the living room and we ran back into the kitchen, knowing it was time to leave.

WHOOOO!! WHOOO!

"Is that an owl?" Chris asked. "I don't even want to know. I suddenly feel sick."

"Let's get out of here now!" I said.

The day's events had drained our energy and our nerves frazzled.

"Grab these," I said. I handed two bags from the living room to Chris and when I did, a glove drifted over my head in slow motion, like a gliding bird, and landed behind a potted plant near the picture window. Another glove followed.

Something seemed determined to distract us from ever leaving.

"Stop it," I yelled to the ghost. I was freaking out.

Chris was stupefied and Danny burst out in nervous laughter. I jumped when my cell phone rang.

"Hello? Oh Stan, Hi. ..Yeah." I began to speak hesitantly, clearly out of breath.

Chris motioned to me and said in a low voice that Danny needed to use the bathroom badly and he would stand guard. I nodded for them to go ahead but to be quick.

"Sure, no problem, yes I'll tell the lawyer about our offer as soon as..."

Bang! Thwack!"

"What now?" I shouted, covering my hand over the phone.

The boys came running from the direction of the sound.

"I'll piss outside," Danny shouted and he and Chris ran by me and out the door.

I quickly uncovered the phone with my hand, hoping Stan had not heard what just happened.

"Are you guys okay over there?" Stan asked.

"We had a slight accident, but everything's ok. We were just getting ready to leave when you called," I lied.

"Don't let me keep you," Stan said.

"No problem. "I'll talk to you later, Stan."

When I closed my cell phone, a ball of twine flew at me. *I'm going to have a heart attack,* I thought.

"Ouch!" I screamed.

Chris and Danny came in as a bottle of Elmer's glue hit me in the back.

"Where did that one come from?" Chris asked with concern.

"While you guys were outside, I got hit with those things," I said pointing to the ball of twine and the glue.

"Does the realtor have an offer?" Chris asked.

"He has a guy who's offering $130,000 for this house and I'm frigging taking it," I said. "It's yours, buddy. I don't want this fucking responsibility. I don't give a shit. I don't care if the lawyer wants more. What's it to him? This place can go to hell."

I suddenly stopped the flood of expletives and realized how the profanity and cursing coming from all of us was escalating. We didn't normally talk this way. However, here in this house it seemed we couldn't help ourselves. What raw and negative emotions were we tapping into?

"I think we're already in Hell," Chris said. "I also think that's the best offer you're going to get."

"I know. What do I care? The house isn't mine and I'm not getting anything from it. It's all going to charity." I angrily kicked a box out of my way. "I've had enough!"

"Can you hand me a bottle of water?" Chris asked me, trying to change the subject. He knew how upset I was and wanted me to calm down. Me freaking out at this time wasn't helping and possibly making things worse. It was possible that my emotional distress was making this worse. I handed him a bottle of water and he took the cap off.

"Mm, nothing like a cold drink," Chris said, downing the water quickly.

"They can have this piece of shit," Danny said to no one in particular. "Get this place cleaned up, sold, goodnight, rest in peace, you lived your lives!"

Suddenly, the water bottle was knocked right out of Chris' hand, and thrown across the living room.

"You see how far that thing flew? Good thing there wasn't any water in it," Chris said.

"It's like he's saying F U," I said. "*They* know the house is getting sold and they're so pissed off they're having a temper tantrum."

"You F me and I'll F you," Chris began to rant. "You want to play games?"

A penny went flying.

"Oh boy, a penny, that's worthless just like this house. Why don't you throw something valuable?" Chris asked. "Something we can actually use. Not your dirt, dust, mildew and cat hair."

A cat brush went flying across the room.

"Good, you can hear me! Go clean your own shitty house. We're done."

"I think it's time to leave, I've had enough guys," I said, not wanting us to provoke the spirits any longer.

"Are we done?" Danny asked. "Let's get our stuff and leave NOW, please."

We didn't have to tell Danny twice since he was ready to go out the door. I agreed and we grabbed our stuff and placed it in the kitchen. Then, I went into the dining room, grabbed my purse, looked down and saw three boxes we needed to take with us.

"Take these books," I said to Chris, quickly ushering him out.

"Let's bring these to the library and be done," Danny said. "Good night, rest in peace, you dead shits."

"Holy crap!" Chris screamed. The plastic piece from the vent had come flying again and hit him hard. "Ouch!"

"Oh, my God, are you okay?" I asked.

"Call a demolition crew and have them bulldoze this house," Danny said angrily.

"I'm getting the fuck out of here," Chris said.

"I am too," I said, agreeing with Chris.

"Goodnight to your smelly, fucking, piece of shit house," Chris yelled. Chris had gone too far.

The bottle of cologne flew from the kitchen counter and hit Chris right in the face.

"Stop it! You guys are provoking it," I screamed, "Stop it!"

"Goodnight," Danny yelled again. From behind us came a banshee-like moan.

Danny ran out of the house as kitchen objects began to rain down on us: wooden spoons, a funnel, a pot lid and silverware.

"Get out of there!" Danny yelled to us.

"Let's move, Mom," Chris screamed to me. We ran through the debris while he hit the objects out of our way with a plastic bat he was holding. We ran as fast as we could through the kitchen and met Danny outside in the driveway.

"Are you guys ok?" Danny asked. We were both panting,

I nodded, half out of breath.

Chris looked down, noticing that his brittle plastic bat was broken in half. He threw it to the ground clearly satisfied.

"So when do we get to come here again?" Chris asked, sarcastically.

Chapter 20

THE SKEPTIC GETS HIS DUE

People who hear this story might wonder why we kept going back.

We really didn't want to go back to the house so soon after the terrifying experience we had the day before. Unfortunately, we had left in such a hurry that I had forgotten to take several important items for Paul's cousins in Germany.

The main reason we continued to work, I had to admit, was that I needed the money. I had put too much sweat equity into this estate to turn my back on everything now. I refused to let the ghosts scare me away. I thought that I had earned and deserved whatever percentage of the executor's fee that would come to me when the estate settled.

The lawyer was able to get me an advance on the fee, which was good because I was in desperate need of income. The economic downturn that our country was experiencing had hit my business particularly hard and my son's boss had still cut back his hours. Kent felt bad, but had no choice. Chris and I joked that Paul's estate had become our own economic stimulus package.

Luckily, the next day, Bob was with us to help us clear out more items from the house. He also volunteered to help us with the last shelf of boxes in the basement. I could hardly believe we were almost finished cleaning it out.

Everything started out fine when we met up with Bob, but I could feel that something wasn't right with him. He was usually very

Anita Jo Intenzo

cooperative when he helped us, but that day he seemed a bit combative. I didn't need that kind of an attitude with what I had just been through.

I had a case of frazzled nerves from the day before from all the extreme paranormal activity I had seen along with Chris and Danny. I thought Bob would be more sympathetic to my situation since we had been dating during all this time I was the executor. He knew what I was going through. Bob prided himself on his loyalty to his church and friends, so why couldn't he recognize and appreciate the loyalty I had shown to my deceased friend?

Bob had shown his skepticism before, but I thought that with everything he had witnessed with us at the house that he was more in the camp of believers. His deep religious beliefs were at the center of his life and I admired him for that. I also knew I didn't share his sometimes zealous convictions and that was a sore point for him in our relationship. Our last few times together had been tense as he pressed me to become more conservative in my beliefs to match his and become more active at church. This went against my true nature. Looking back, I realized our relationship was like a ticking time bomb.

Bob was walking down the stairs from one of his trash runs when he was hit in the neck with something. Chris found a tan spool of thread on the floor near the steps.

Chris showed it to him. "It was this, Bob."

He didn't seem to believe Chris or think it was any big deal.

"Come on Bob, you don't think that it's crazy that you just got hit in the neck?" I asked

"I'm not afraid," Bob said. "The Lord will protect me."

Great, I thought, I guess Chris and I are on our own.

About a half hour later, Chris and Bob were coming down the stairs with Chris walking behind Bob when I suddenly heard Chris yell, "Duck!"

A wooden painter's stick came out of nowhere and flew right at them. They both ducked in time and the stick landed on the other side of the staircase with a loud thud.

"Jesus!" yelled Chris. "Did you see that?"

124

"I don't know what that was." Bob said. He didn't seem disturbed by the poltergeist activity, but was upset about Chris taking the Lord's name in vain.

Chris rolled his eyes at me and told Bob he was sorry he had offended him. I couldn't believe the way Bob was acting. Maybe if a sofa fell on him he might be convinced. I tried to stay calm and not let his skepticism affect me and went back to the last remaining boxes on the corner shelf. Bob stood near me and I handed him a trash bag. I had failed to mention to him that small random objects were being thrown my way too, although they were more gentle in nature - a small Greek doll and slides when I was throwing out moldy VHS tapes.

"Anita, I have to tell you that I'm having a hard time understanding the meaning of all this. Maybe it's because you're just exhausted and are seeing things," Bob said.

Chris immediately protested the absurdity of what he had just heard. "Dude, you should have been here yesterday."

"How can you say that?" I asked. "You've been here from the beginning of the poltergeist activity. *Now* you don't want to believe what you've seen. Fine, but don't think what's going on in this house is happening because I'm exhausted. I'm not hallucinating or imagining it all. Chris and I have been at this long enough to know this place is definitely haunted by ghosts and one of them is my friend, Paul." I was angry and turned away from him.

"Yeah, but how do you know it's your friend?"

Just as Bob said that, I felt something hit me in the back of the neck. I looked down at the ground and picked up a small off-white square piece of plastic. I turned it over and saw it was a name badge, which I had never seen before. On it was embossed the name, *Paul Jaeger, Susquehanna University.*

"That's how," I said. "Any questions?" I showed him the badge. He was so shocked that words failed him.

Chapter 21

SEEING RED

PING!

"What was that?" I asked Kent and Chris.

We were in the cat room moving the sewing machine from against the wall. He and Chris were going to carry it into the living room so Paul's niece could pick it up in a few days.

"I think it's still connected, there's the plug in the back," I said to Kent as we knelt on the floor. Chris grabbed the camcorder he had brought in case we were lucky to capture something while his boss was here. We still had so much to go through in the room, and Chris wanted to document any paranormal activity on film with a witness present. When Kent unplugged the cord from the back wall, something large and red came down near his ear. It hit the bottom of the metal stand of the floor lamp with a loud ping. The look on Kent's face was a priceless mixture of stunned surprise, concern and astonishment.

"Something red flashed near you guys," Chris said. "It came from behind me and landed in that corner."

We quickly searched the corner and Kent found it.

"A comb," Kent said holding it up.

"Huh?" I said.

"It's a giant red comb in the shape of a fish," Chris said.

We had no idea where the comb had come from, as we had never seen it before.

"That comb was really weird," Kent said.

"That's nothing," I replied. "Welcome to our crazy world!"

"I'm going to look around while you show Kent what we have left to do," Chris said.

Chris walked into the living room and I showed Kent the bedrooms.

"What's that smell?" Kent asked.

Chris walked into the hallway with the camera. "Yuck, smells like wet cat."

"It's pungent as hell," Kent said.

"God, it's awful," I said.

While Chris walked around the house, I left my tape recorder on in the living room, hoping to get some EVPs. Chris continued to walk around with his camera.

"Look at all this," Chris said to the camera.

The living room was still jammed with boxes, paintings, and other things for Carl.

"I'll take this TV," Kent said.

"Sure, take it, by all means," I said. "There's only five more in the house."

"Here, take the camera from me for a minute," Chris said.

He picked up the box and went outside leaving me alone. I walked around with the camera, and out of the corner of my eye, I saw the motion detector light blink several times, as if someone had walked by it. Kent and Chris came back inside a short time later.

"What?" Chris asked me when he saw the puzzled look on my face.

"I saw the motion detector light blinking like crazy and I wasn't anywhere near it."

Kent was intrigued. "Is it supposed to do that?"

"It's on sensitive mode right now," Chris explained. "The beam stays solid yellow until something crosses in front of it, then it sets off the alarm but it won't go off while we are in the house. Mom has to activate that each time we leave."

"Chris, Kent, let's stand way over here and see what it does."

We stood still, out of the beam's direction, and it stayed solid yellow. After a few more minutes I said, "I don't know, maybe I'm seeing things."

"Well, let's just keep an eye on it later," Chris said, "How about we tackle the kitchen now."

We made our way to the kitchen and a magic marker hit me in the back.

"Gotcha," Kent said, trying to lighten the mood.

Chris laughed.

"I owe you one, Kent." I said.

"Yes you do!" Kent said. "Hey, did you clean out these cabinets yet?

"Not completely, but first let's pack...." I never finished my sentence.

Suddenly we heard a smack, like something slapping against the wall. We ran from the kitchen to find a red felt-tip pen that must have come out of the cat room and hit the adjacent wall

Chris walked to the back hall and we stayed in the living room hoping to see something else.

"You wanna fight?" Chris asked, picking up a stick.

"No, don't do that," I said. "Don't provoke them, it's not right."

"We should put the camera down and set it in one direction," I said. "That way if we leave a room we won't miss anything."

"First, help me bring this one other thing out to my car," Kent said to Chris. They lifted a square wooden pedestal. "Thanks, Anita. This will be great to display things in the lobby."

"Glad you can use it, Kent, it's another heavy thing out of my way."

Chris and Kent carried it outside to the van and I stayed in the living room with the camera. I began to ask some questions aloud while keeping an eye on the motion detector, making sure I wasn't in its path.

"Are you upset we are taking things? Are you here, Paul? Give us a sign?"

Blink, went the motion detector. Had something crossed its path?

CLANG!

"Whoa," I heard Chris say as he came into the kitchen.

"What just happened?" I asked.

"Something flew across the dining room, like a red blur," Chris said.

"I just asked them to do something," I told Chris.

"When I was about halfway into the kitchen I saw this red blur go diagonally across the door frame," Chris explained to me.

Kent and I searched for the object as I handed the camera back to Chris. We couldn't find anything.

"I don't know about this place. I was skeptical in the beginning but that comb *still* kind of freaks me out," Kent said.

"Everyone has that one experience that stands out and makes a real impression on them," I told Kent. "In your case it's that red comb."

"Yeah, but why is everything red? Is there some significance with that color?" Kent asked.

"I think it may have been one of Mrs. Jaeger's favorite colors," I stated.

"Does that mean she's here?" Kent asked me.

I couldn't answer that.

I looked around and wondered. *Was Mrs. Jaeger present?*

Kent was now holding the camera for Chris for a moment.

"Anyone want to have some fun?" Chris asked.

"Are you ready for some fantasy football?" Kent asked, laughing.

"I am. Anyone else interested?" Chris asked as he turned to me.

"Not me, I'm more interested in you two helping finish in this living room."

Kent handed the camera back to Chris and noticed some religious items, which Paul had left to a convent in his will. "These are the things that we packed for the nuns," I said to Kent. "Now they told me they don't want them. I mean, it's a convent full of elderly nuns. What are they going to do with these old VHS tapes?"

"You're right. They probably want DVDs instead," Kent, joked.

"No, they want Blu-ray!" Chris joked back. "It's like 'hey, I got *Passion of the Christ* on Blu-ray, the hell with VHS!'"

At that point, we all started laughing.

"I guess the Lord in High Def is a must," Chris said.

"I want *The Ten Commandments* on Blu-ray." Kent joked back again.

A slide flew right over our heads.

"We did it this time, guys," I said. "We are being disrespectful." I picked up the slide and looked at it. "I think it's a slide of the Holy Land. No, it's a bridge in Italy."

"Is it a bridge over troubled water?" Kent asked sarcastically.

"It's the famed Venetian Bridge," I said. "What do I do with this, Paul?" I put down the slide. "And now I'll have to get rid of all this religious stuff!"

How about giving it to a library or a gift shop?" Kent asked

I was completely frustrated. "Maybe," I said.

"Anita, you should have a yard sale and get rid of it all in one shot for fifty cents each."

Another slide went flying, hitting Kent.

"What was that?" Kent asked.

"It's a slide of some carved relief of ... I think... Mayan Indian," I replied holding it up to the light. "See, he's mad, he doesn't want his stuff sold for fifty cents."

"That slide sailed right over your head, Chris, from the direction of the dining room," Kent said half laughing, not believing what he just saw.

"I caught that on tape," said Chris.

Later as we sat at the dining room table to have some refreshments, we pointed the camera into the living room so we didn't miss anything.

"Wouldn't it be funny if something came out of the tape," Kent said. Then he whistled a creepy tune.

"Like what, Kent? Like some stupid monster hand...in 3D? Please," I said as I rolled my eyes and had the thought; *please don't give the ghosts any ideas.*

"Do you know that the drawer is full of slides, Anita?" Kent asked as he took a look in the buffet.

"Maybe that's where they all are coming from," I said.

We finished our little break and Chris got a call on his cell and walked into the kitchen. Kent and I stacked some boxes in the living room and chatted about the house.

"They're coming down on Wednesday to see the house, Mom," Chris called out to me, still on the phone.

"My cousin and her daughters are coming down," I told Kent. "I should start selling tickets."

"Son of a no-good bastard!" Chris yelled from the kitchen.

"What happened?" I asked running in.

"Something hit me in the face when I hung up the phone," Chris explained to us. He looked around the countertop near the sink. "I think it was that red cork over there that hit me. It smacked me right in the cheek and then hit the wall."

We could see a red welt where it hit Chris' cheek.

"The camera's dead," I said picking it up. "That didn't take long."

Kent hooked up an extension cord to the camera. We had brought this in case the batteries went dead and now I realized that was a good decision. We walked back into the living room and while we stood there and listened to the finished tape recording, a red pen hit Chris in the hand.

"Stop throwing stuff at me, you weirdoes," Chris yelled.

"What just hit me in the neck?" I asked. I looked around and found a rather large safety pin on the floor near me. "This is it. That had a lot of force behind it and really hurt."

"Have you guys been getting hit more with things recently?" Kent asked.

I turned to him. "It's been escalating," I said. "There are so many things around here for them to throw," I said.

I noticed some dishes and cups by the sink that I wanted to pack up and I asked Kent if he wanted any of them.

"Thanks, I could use some for the office," Kent replied. "Anita, how can you just go about your business while all this weird stuff is happening around you?" he asked.

"Someone's has to do it and as executor, it's my job. Besides it's what Paul wanted and he was my friend."

"That's what I don't understand? Kent said. "He wanted you to do this for him and now he's haunting you not to do it?"

"Maybe he changed his mind. Can you do that when you're dead?"

It was a question no one could answer.

Kent held the camera once again as Chris and I packed up some last things in the kitchen. Chris handed me some more old newspaper to wrap dishes safely when he picked up the obituaries section.

"They say if you don't see your name in here, it's a good day," Chris told to Kent and the camera.

YOU KNNNNOOOOW IT!!!!

We all stood frozen to the spot, stunned by the eerie voice coming from the living room area.

"I think it's time to go when you hear people from beyond start answering you," Kent stated.

"If the floating slides didn't freak you out, then *that* will!" I said. "We'll be out of here soon. Let's get these last things wrapped up and go."

Are you dead?

It sounded like a child's voice and it came from the same area as the other supernatural voice.

"Did I just hear that right?" I asked.

We tried to finish quickly. It was weird that the voices were so different from each other, one a man and one a child.

"Here! Have an orange squeezer," I said trying to lighten the mood. Chris laughed.

"This is an ancient cereal bowl that gets thrown out."

We all laughed at the absurd sentence I just uttered.

A metal ring appeared out of nowhere, and went flying over our heads and landed on the top of the refrigerator.

"They must not want their things thrown out," Kent said still recording all of this.

Chris climbed on a chair, and found a thin silver metal bangle bracelet on the refrigerator and showed it to me.

"I've never seen this before, Chris," I said. "This bracelet came out of the thin air and landed on top of the fridge."

Shortly after Chris walked into the living room to get me another box, we heard a loud bang. Chris yelled out, "What the hell?"

"What's wrong?" Kent asked as he and I ran into the living room. We were just in time to see a bright shimmering white light fly over Chris' head, land on the wall and then disappeared into it. "Did you guys SEE THAT?"

The motion detector's light was now blinking rapidly, but no one was in the beam's path.

"Kent did you get that on film?" I asked.

We had.

CLANG!

We heard a metal sound coming from the kitchen.

"Oh Jeez!" I said and went into the kitchen. "It's the metal orange squeezer."

"First the loud bang and now the metal squeezer," Chris said.

Chris took a seat in the kitchen catching his breath and sipped some iced tea. I continued to pack up the rest of the stuff as quickly as possible while Kent continued to record everything that was happening from the dining room. Chris watched me, shaking his head.

"I still can't figure out where that bracelet came from before," I said to Chris.

"It's old," Kent said. "It's from the past, past times...Past Images by Anita." Kent panned to my large business card on the fridge. Paul had proudly put up my new magnetized business card a few months before he died.

Suddenly, a dark glove hit the refrigerator in front of Kent.

"Where did that come from?" Kent asked half laughing, "I think I got half of it on camera."

"It hit my Mom's business card," Chris said.

"You did that," Kent said

"I did not!" Chris exclaimed. "I'm sitting here drinking my tea and the glove came from back here on the table, flew over my head and hit her card. I swear on her life!" He pointed at me.

"Gee, thanks!" I said.

"Welcome to the haunted kitchen!" Chris said to the camera. "Things that go bump in broad daylight!"

BANG!

Chris got up quickly and went into the living room to search for whatever made the noise. It sounded like something hit the hall closet door.

"Is this new?" Chris asked from the living room. He held up a big converter plug." I think this is what hit the door."

"That definitely would have made a loud bang." I said

"Should I stop filming since we are getting ready to go?" Kent asked.

"They do things right up to when we leave sometimes," I said. "I would leave it on."

Suddenly, I remembered the bucket downstairs had to be emptied; I really didn't want to go down there alone.

"One more thing," I said. "Who wants to come down with me to empty the bucket of water?"

"I'll go down with you," Chris said. "I ain't afraid of no ghosts."

Kent stayed upstairs with the camera, finishing out the tape.

We emptied the bucket. The old, clogged double sinks were removed when the sump pump was constructed, so there was nowhere for the air conditioner's condensation pipe to drain. It was a makeshift solution and the new homeowners would have to correct this problem in the future.

"Chris, make sure you hit the lights on the way up," I said.

He switched them off and as we began to walk upstairs a painter's stick went flying over our heads

"Jesus Christ, I think it's time to go." Chris said.

We were hurrying up the stairs when a miniature statue of Jesus flew over our heads, up the stairs and out the kitchen door. We couldn't believe what just happened!

More loud sounds came from the basement.

"I'll go down and see," Chris replied. "Have Kent keep the camera on me."

I was curious as well and followed Chris down the steps.

"Watch out!" Chris yelled.

A seashell flew at my head and I ducked just in time.

"Kent, come down here with the camera!" Chris called to him.

BANG!

"Oh my God," I screamed. "That was so loud!"

A big scrub brush was violently tossed across the room.

"That took a lot of strength to pick that...ahhh...ewww...it's in my mouth," Chris said. "There are cobwebs are all over me. I'm wrapped in them. All in my mouth too, how disgusting!"

Kent came down with the camera as more items flew around the basement. He plugged the cord into the one outlet that worked and a cassette tape of *Hello Dolly* in German landed on the floor.

CRASH!

A small stepladder fell down.

"I'm getting it all," Kent said.

"The cobwebs are all over the basement," Chris said. "I can't escape them. I'm completely covered. You know, ghosts, I'm tired of your slime."

Kent and I saw no cobwebs. "Come on, let's go," I said. "Enough is enough."

"It looks like we are going to be dealing with this type of activity, on and off until this place gets sold."

"Unfortunately," Kent said, "I think Chris is right."

"The question is," I hesitated, "who's going to last longer, the ghosts or us?"

Chapter 22

CREEPED OUT COUSINS

One of the reasons that my cousin Lisa and her two daughters wanted to see the "haunted house" was an incident that occurred one Friday night before their visit.

Lisa's daughter, Faith, drove down from her home to visit my son on that Friday night. Chris and his friends had invited her to a local club to hear one of their favorite bands.

She and I caught up on how her family was while Chris went upstairs to change from his work clothes. I asked her about a recent trip she and her Mom had taken to Williamsburg, Virginia that past month. Faith said they had a wonderful time and then commented about how beautiful Williamsburg was. While we talked, Chris came out to the patio where we were sitting and handed me four photo slides.

"These were on my bed," he said. "I know when I made my bed this morning they weren't on my bedspread."

"What are they of?" I asked.

"Take a look," he said.

I held them up to the light, looked closely and recognized two interior shots of what looked like colonial workrooms. There were two other slides, one of a large mansion, and the other of my friend Paul as a little boy sitting on Santa Claus' lap.

"Faith, check this out," I said. "I think these are of Colonial Williamsburg. That's the Governor's Palace, isn't it?"

Faith looked at them. "Yes, that's the Governor's Palace and that looks like the Blacksmith's shop and I think that's the Potter's shop. We bought a blue and gray pitcher in their gift shop. This is really strange."

"While you were upstairs we were talking about Williamsburg," I said to Chris.

"Paul must have heard you since he's in one of the slides," Chris said. "What else could it be?"

Faith called her mother on her cell phone and told her what had just happened. Apparently, Chris had already told her a few things about the house when they talked on the phone before her visit.

When she got off the phone, Faith turned to us. "My mom and sister would like to come down sometime to see the house, if it's okay with you. She just loves *Ghost Hunters*."

I looked at Chris ruefully. "I don't know if that's a good idea. It's not a safe place and I don't want anyone to get hurt," I said.

Chris looked at me. "It's your call, Mom."

"We'll have to see," I said.

Chris' friends showed up to go to the club. I made the boys promise to look out for Faith, and then told them to have a good time. After they left, I hoped that I wouldn't be asked about going to the house again. However, it seemed the lure of a haunted house was too much for my cousin and her daughters to resist.

—m—

Days later, my relatives came to the house. They hoped to catch some paranormal activity with their camera since they were big fans of the ghost shows on TV. I was annoyed and told Chris that Paul's house wasn't a venue for entertainment. I had even told Lisa that we could not guarantee any ghostly activity, that there were days when nothing happened. That didn't deter them from coming to the house, even at the risk to their own safety. Chris had his camera while walking around with Karen, exploring a couple of the main rooms. I was showing Lisa around, telling her some of the back-story about the Jaegers, and some of the crazy things we had experienced over the last few months. Just as Faith came out of the bathroom, a small stepladder slammed against the adjacent wall.

Faith screamed. "What the hell was that?"

"They're just letting us know they're here," Chris replied.

Chris moved the ladder as Lisa and I came over to see what happened.

"Put the ladder in Paul's room," I said. "We don't need anyone getting hurt today."

They were already clearly freaked out by the first sign of activity. Faith had on a black t-shirt that said "Ghosts of Williamsburg" on it and Chris was the first one to notice it.

He laughed. "Got ghosts, cuz?"

Faith replied, "Yeah, apparently we do."

Lisa and I were in Paul's room and I was explaining to her how cluttered it used to be, when a mirror came crashing down in the hallway.

"Is everyone ok?" I asked as I picked up the mirror and stood it back up against the wall. "Thank God no one was in the hallway when it fell.

"This is incredible," Karen said with delight. "Two incidents within minutes of each other and we've only been here for twenty minutes."

"What is that smell?" Lisa asked. "It stinks of wet cat."

The smell was overpowering. Then it vanished.

Chris began to walk to the basement door. "Who wants to come downstairs with me?"

"Me, me," Karen agreed quickly.

They headed downstairs with the camcorder in the hope of catching something on tape. I stayed upstairs with Lisa and Faith and we talked about Colonial Williamsburg.

"Paul loved going to Williamsburg and was a huge supporter of their history programs," I said. "In fact he left money to their foundation."

"Have you tried contacting those paranormal investigators on TV and telling them your story?" Lisa asked as she cautiously looked around the room.

"In fact, we did. I contacted several on their web sites and only *Ghost Hunters* got back to me the next day."

Lisa got excited when I told her this. "Are they coming here to investigate?"

"I heard from their case manager, Kris, and she was very nice in her e-mail back to me. Unfortunately, they are so booked up they couldn't schedule an investigation on such short notice before the house gets sold. So we're contacting another group," I said. "I'll let you know what happens."

Lisa suddenly jumped a foot towards me and screamed.

"What's wrong?" Faith asked her.

"Oh, my God, something freezing cold just touched my elbow!" she exclaimed half-laughing, half terrified.

"It's probably Paul," I said. "He's acknowledging the fact that we're talking about Williamsburg." We could both feel the cold draft where we were standing.

—⁂—

"Get some pictures and I'll follow behind you," Chris said to Karen.

"Ok, what have you guys been getting down here?" Karen asked.

"Well, things being thrown around by ghosts, besides other things."

"Do you think we'll get anything else today?"

"It's very possible. Why don't you ask some questions?" Chris turned his camera on.

"Is there anyone down here?" Karen asked. "Do you care that your stuff is gone? Give us a holler back."

A few second later, they heard a bang.

"That sounded like something hit that brown bag over there," Chris said, pointing to the corner of the room. "Oh...wow... look. It's a bottle of whiteout."

Karen gasped. "I saw that all the way over there a couple of minutes ago," she said, pointing to a shelf on the other side of the basement. "My camera just died."

Squeak.

"What was that?" Chris and Karen asked simultaneously.

"Sounded like a seal or maybe a bird," Chris said.

They walked over in the direction of the sound and Karen noticed a picture on the bookshelf. "Is that the Mom?"

"No, that's Julie Andrews," Chris replied. "Paul really liked her."

"Oh, well, now he got to meet her," Karen said.

Chris laughed. "She isn't *dead*."

"Oh," Karen said, "Sorry, my bad."

CLANG!

Something metallic slammed against the ceiling directly above them. Karen screamed and went flying up the stairs and Chris looked across the basement.

"What the hell was that?" Chris yelled. "It sounded like metal pipe being ripped off the wall.

We heard the sound from upstairs and saw Karen running towards us. I yelled down the steps to Chris, asked if he was okay, and decided we needed to stay together. Karen composed herself and walked back down with us where we found Chris looking on the floor to see if anything had fallen. Karen found it first.

"A fucking spool," she said. She held it up.

"It looks like a copper pipe fitting," Chris said.

Lisa jumped up and hurried towards Chris. "Oh, my God Chris, save me."

"What's the matter?"

"Something just grabbed the back of my leg,"

"You ok?"

"Yes, but... no."

Chris explained to us what had happened while we were upstairs getting everyone up to speed.

"A little red ball just hit me," Karen said. "Then something hit my ponytail. Ok, ghosts, I believe you're here. You don't have to convince me anymore."

I showed Lisa and Faith around and Chris and Karen walked over to the other side of the basement.

"That was so crazy," Karen said. "I can't get over what just happened and the fact that it happened to me."

"I can't find anything that would have made such a loud noise," Chris said.

"That's strange," Karen said, scratching her head. "Hey Mom, I found a cane for you." Her mother narrowed her eyes at her as if to say, "I'm not *that* old."

"She wouldn't want that, it's famous," Chris said.

Chris and Karen walked over to us, with her proudly holding up the cane.

"It's the famous dancing cane," I said, and told them the story about it.

"If it's haunted, I don't want it," Lisa said.

"Sounds like it could have been a Goosebumps book," Chris joked. "It's *The Haunted Dancing Cane.*"

Karen put the cane back and showed Faith around the basement while Chris continued to film. A small shoe went sailing by.

"This could be on Funniest Home Videos." Chris continued to joke. "Gimme your baby shoe!"

Chris laughed loudly as Karen and Faith stood frozen.

"It's so tiny," Faith said, looking at the baby shoe.

"I wear it every night!" Chris joked.

"I hope you don't hurt yourself," Faith said.

"Looks like the ghosts are having fun with us today," Karen said.

"I have never in my life..." Lisa began. "If I ever doubted you, Anita, I swear, I would testify in open court that there is something going on." She hugged me.

"Everyone has their own experiences," I said. "Even if it's just one thing that happens to you, that's the thing that will stay with you. It's very personal the way it touches you. Lisa got touched today."

"How sweet," Chris said.

Lisa sneered at him. Chris walked around with Karen and took some more pictures. I showed Lisa and Faith some dusty history books that I had found.

"You're welcome to what's here. The library didn't want them."

Ping! Bang!

"That was the washer," Chris said. "It sounded like someone ran right into it."

"What's this?" Karen asked. "There's a magnet on the side of the washer."

It read: *You have a friend in Pennsylvania!*

"That magnet was never there before," Chris said.

"I should take it and put it on my fridge," Karen said.

"Be my guest and have some ghost memorabilia," Chris said.

A music cassette flew across the room. Chris documented the thrown tape and walked over to Faith.

"Have you had any experiences today?" Chris asked her.

"You're damn right, I did."

"Did anyone touch you?" Chris asked.

"No, and they better not, if they know what's good for them."

"There are cobwebs all over me," Karen said, as she tried to brush off all the invisible threads.

"Wait, I did get something," Faith said looking at the camera. "I got a black shadow ghost or creature thing in my picture." She showed it to me.

"You're right," I said. "It's half peering around the back corner of that wardrobe. That's where we picked up a reflection of a shadow man before. You are going to have to send me a copy of that."

Karen walked back over to us. "You feel cobwebs?"

"You're getting them too, huh," Chris said. "It's gross isn't it? That's your creepy experience for the day. Anything happen with you personally today, Mom?"

"No, I think I have had enough experiences," I laughed.

Chris zeroed in on a plastic lawn gnome on a shelf, and trying to lighten the mood said, "Hey, it's the Travelocity guy!"

"Looks just like him," Faith said, "It's so funny."

We all laughed for a minute until Chris made jokes at the ghosts again.

"Move the can jackass!"

"Chris! I will personally rearrange your butt if something happens now," Lisa said.

"That would be uncomfortable," Karen said.

Chris and Karen laughed and walked off together. "Let's go find dead people on this side of the basement."

I brought out another box of books for Lisa and Faith to look through. Lisa bent over to look through the books as a paintbrush hit her.

"Oh my God, oh my God!" Faith said repeatedly.

"Why are you screaming?" Lisa asked her daughter, "It hit *me*."

Lisa began to cry and laugh at the same time.

"This is so not fun anymore," Faith said frozen.

I held up the paintbrush. "See that, Chris?"

"I got it," Chris said. "I see you're taking their books!"

"We'll take good care of them," Lisa said to the air. "I love books."

They would be sorry later about taking the books and other items when they experienced paranormal activity that they attributed to what they'd taken. Lisa's husband, although professing himself a non-believer, even made them throw everything out in the trash. It was that serious.

"I told you this house is not for the faint of heart," I said.

After they calmed down, I showed them some other things in the basement. "Here are some sweater coats if you can use them, Lisa. All you have to do is wash them, they're brand new," I told her. We all stayed in one area with Chris filming.

"What is that?" Chris jerked back with his camera as something flew by him. "It was white, I don't know, it landed on the box."

We searched around and found nothing. I told them about the phantom phone calls and other events that happened previously as they listened intently.

"Chris, that bottle of whiteout is gone from where I put it," Karen said.

"Really?" Chris said.

"It's gone!" Lisa exclaimed. "The whiteout is gone. I saw Karen put it there and now it's gone!"

"Maybe that's the white thing I saw flew by," Chris said.

"Did you look behind those boxes?" Karen asked pointing to the shelves.

"Let me see," I said.

I went over and moved the boxes and there, sitting on a shelf, was the bottle of whiteout.

Everyone was stunned at what just happened.

A few minutes later, I went about business as usual. I was used to all this. "Do you guys need hangers?" I asked, trying to act normal. Who was I kidding?

"I felt something," Karen said. "Something just grabbed me. That was gross, like a slimy hand or something."

A broom flew across the room and hit some shelves.

"Damn, there is a major cold spot over here now," Chris said placing his hand near the sump pump drain.

"I feel it too," Karen said. Should we explore over here?"

"I guess," Chris sighed, suddenly feeling tired.

Karen moved a chair to sit on by one of the walls. "Film me Chris," she said.

"Ok, no problem," Chris said.

Karen sat on the chair as he took pictures behind her.

"Hey Chris, this is creepy," Karen said.

"What do you have?"

She showed him her picture of a man's profile standing behind her!

"Show that to everyone," Chris said.

Karen walked over and showed us the picture as we were going through some more boxes.

"That's creepy as hell!" I said.

Chris jumped and grabbed his shoulder. "Whoa, an icy hand grabbed my shoulder!"

"Because we are moving new stuff today," I said.

"That's new alright," Chris said. "We have people touching and grabbing us. I don't know if I like that!"

"Oh look, a book on the *Tower of London*," Faith said. "Anne Boleyn's ghost is said to be there. Maybe your friend is hanging out with *her* now."

Then we heard a rapid knocking sound coming from a pipe above us.

"Is that a yes?" I asked.

"Maybe we should go upstairs," Karen said nervously.

"There's a lot of stuff still going on down here and we may miss something," Chris said.

Karen reluctantly agreed and took some more pictures of the chair in the same position as before but this time nothing supernatural showed up in the picture.

"Strange, isn't it Chris?" Karen asked.

Chris nodded. "Hey, you guys do what you have to do, I'm going to sit down and film. My back hurts."

Karen went over to sit and talk with Chris and a few minutes later Faith called them. "Come over here guys. I'm getting orbs on my camera."

We all ran over to Faith who had apparently captured some pictures of orbs in the basement even though we couldn't see them with the naked eye.

It now seemed that whatever was throwing things had calmed down a bit. We talked a bit more about what we were experiencing, when Chris said he felt he was being led back over to the other side of the basement.

"Look, there are more slides are all over the floor," he said.

Chris sat down again on the chair. Karen joined him. "Those slides weren't on the floor when we were over here before," she said. "Ouch! Something pinched me on the back of my leg." Karen jumped up from the chair. "Now it feels like cobwebs are wrapped all around it."

"Yeah, I feel them on my legs too."

Lisa and I went through the rest of the sweaters while Faith went around the basement with her camera.

BANG!

A silver pocketknife flew by us and hit the ground. Faith came running over.

CRASH!

Just then another cassette tape went flying across the room and hit the floor.

"And I thought I was going to be bored," Karen said to Chris.

"Those damn cobwebs again," Karen said. "They just won't stop."

"They're all over the place," Chris replied. "I can't wait to be done with this place."

Lisa, Faith and I didn't experience any cobwebs at our end of the basement.

SMASH!

A pillbox flew by on our side of the basement.

"Great, break that now," I said. "I could have used that."

"All your stuff belongs to us," Karen said, taunting them.

CRASH!

"Jesus Christ!" I screamed running over to Chris and Karen. "It sounded like a whole shelf came down."

Nothing was there. Nothing was on the ground. We found nothing that could have made the loud noise.

"I thought for sure something had fallen," I said. "It sounded so real!"

"This is ridiculous." Chris said. "Phantom sounds now?"

"Hey, why are you throwing stuff at me?" Faith exclaimed suddenly. "I'm not touching your damn books anymore! I'm sorry! He just threw that piece of wood at me. I'm done looking at your books. You can kiss my butt."

A wooden dowel fell down in front of us, making us all jump and scream. Chris and Karen had both gotten it on camera. Faith, Lisa and I gathered the clothes together to take upstairs as Chris and Karen walked around for one final sweep of the basement. Then we heard a loud slam. A big metal bolt hit the side of the metal filing cabinet denting the side.

Chris came back over to us with the camera.

"I'm putting this in my pocket so you can't throw it anymore," I yelled. "You damn jackass! You could have killed someone with this!"

"Why would you throw a bolt anyway? Karen asked. "Someone is mad. Is that you? What's his father's name?"

"Hans," I answered.

"Is that you, Hans?"

Another pocketknife flew across the room.

"Having fun?" I asked.

A cassette tape titled *Princess Grace* went flying.

"I'm taking this goddamn thing!" I said.

A film cartridge went flying.

"What the fuck?" Chris asked. "The fucking film almost hit me."

The obscenities started again.

I picked up the film cartridge, threw it back on the ground and stomped on it. "This is what I think of your film!" I exclaimed. "Look, it won't even break. What a piece of shit! I am so tired of all this bullshit that I have been dealing with for months." I had tried to remain calm but I was tired and fed-up.

Chris filmed me as I stomped on the film while everyone pointed and laughed. "Show them who is boss, Mom," he said.

Tapes and slides were thrown near us once again as Chris filmed. Then we heard a bang over on the other side and Chris went to investigate. We started throwing out some of the objects that had been flying at us and then heard more bangs from Chris' side of the basement.

"They're revving up," I said. "This can't be good."

"Everything is coming from this one side," Chris said, as he walked to the back of the staircase with his camera.

"What's that? OH JESUS CHRIST!" Suddenly, Chris jumped and ran straight forward, crashing into the wooden studs that were all that was left of the wall partition, taking part of it with him as he fell to the ground. He didn't know it at the time, but he had caught, on film, a snake-like shadow cast against the wall, crawling up thin air.

"Chris....Chris...." I screamed, "What happened?"

Chris brushed himself off and he got up from the floor. We huddled around him to see if he was hurt. He checked his camera to see if it was broken. It wasn't.

"Something crawled up my back and tried to wrap itself around my neck," he looked pale and shaken. "Son of a bitch...I hurt my leg."

Karen quickly looked around and found a five-foot long gray cord near Chris' feet. "It was this," she stated, as she looked at the shelf near the steps. "I saw that cord before and it was lying coiled on the shelf."

We were horrified. Something had deliberately attacked Chris. Karen touched my arm and said in a shaky, pleading voice, "Come on Anita, let's get out of here."

Once upstairs, we quickly gathered our things to go, and stopped in our tracks as we heard the disembodied voice of woman.

"GEEEET OUUUUT!"

I swear it was Hilda Jaeger's voice.

We all bolted for the door and my cousin and her daughters ran for their car. They quickly said goodbye and drove off. They never asked to come and see the house again.

Chapter 23

BIRTHDAY SURPRISE

I could have thought of a hundred ways to spend my birthday rather than showing Paul's house to prospective buyers. Nevertheless, that's exactly what I was doing. After a quick birthday dinner at my parents' house, Chris and I drove to the house to meet the realtor, Stan, who had a couple with him interested in buying the house "as is."

The day before, Chris and I had cleaned up as best we could, but there were still boxes stacked in one corner for Paul's brother. We expected to finish clearing out the house in nine months and told that to the potential buyers.

I showed them the hall and the bedrooms while Chris kept an eye out for ghostly shenanigans. We had no idea what we were stirring up with new people looking around the house. Our instincts proved to be right.

Several minutes later as we walked back through the living room, Chris caught my eye.

"Why don't you take them downstairs, Mom, and show them the big basement?" He rolled his eyes in the direction of the basement and I knew something was up.

I quickly agreed and took them downstairs. They were quite impressed by the size of the basement and said it might make a great media room.

After ten minutes, we came upstairs to the kitchen and I led them out the side porch door with Stan guiding them to the garage and garden house.

I turned to Chris. "What's going on?" I asked.

"I heard voices and there's other crazy stuff going on in the living room."

"Like what?"

"The small portable TV that was on the side table was moved to the middle of the living room. I moved it back right before you came in," Chris said.

"I'll try and keep them outside for now. It's only a 'walk through' tonight. They'll have to come back if they decide to make an offer," I said.

"I'll stay here and make sure nothing gets thrown past the door," he said.

I felt that I was in some kind of "B" horror movie. I could feel the sweat running down my blouse. Stress was becoming my constant companion. *Cue the spooky music right now,* I thought.

I talked with Stan and his clients for about fifteen minutes and was relieved when they finally left. Stan said he would be in touch with me in the next few days.

Chris met me at the kitchen door. He had been at his post the whole time, "You have to see this to believe it!" he said.

In the kitchen, we found a trail of slides leading into the living room.

"What the hell is this?" I asked.

When I entered the living room, I saw that the place looked like a cyclone had hit it. There were pillows, hangers, a red lid to a container, slides, paper clips and pens everywhere.

"I think they're upset the house is being shown for sale," Chris said.

"Too bad," I yelled. "You're annoyed? Look at this place."

Chris laughed. "Maybe the ghosts are just saying "Happy Birthday."

"Yeah. Happy Birthday to me! That's real funny. Looks like they already had a party and I wasn't invited."

—∭—

I was becoming a target for bad news.

I hadn't heard from Bob in almost a week and my birthday had come and gone without him acknowledging it. No card, no call, there was nothing.

"I'd call him, Mom, and find out what the deal is," my son told me.

"I don't know what's wrong. I talked to him the weekend after he helped us at the house and knew my birthday was coming up. He said he'd be in touch."

"For a guy who wanted to buy you a car and now he doesn't even send you a birthday card, I'd say you have the right to some answers," Chris said. "Stop second guessing him and call him."

Chris was right.

I took a deep breath and made the call.

Bob answered the phone and after a brief exchange, I immediately sensed that he had been holding back his true feelings for weeks.

"I didn't think you wanted to be in touch with me anymore,' Bob said.

"I think there's been a misunderstanding, Bob. I don't remember saying anything like that the last time we were together." I searched my memory and was able to put together an image of the last time we were together and what we said to each other.

"Bob, the last thing I said to you was that I wasn't going to be at the house on Wednesday. I told you not to worry about helping me out that day. You said 'ok, I'll talk to you sometime at the end of the week.' Then, I said, 'great I'll talk to you then.'"

That was it. We hadn't left with angry words or anything. I knew this for certain, because I could totally recall the scene. That's why I was confused when I hadn't heard from him. I hadn't a clue what was on his mind.

Bob remembered a completely different scenario, but I suspected it was his way of starting a confrontation perhaps weeks in the making.

"I think this job at your friend's house has brought to light how different we are, Anita," he began. "You and I are miles apart in our religious convictions."

Here we go, I thought, I knew this was it all along.

"I think your lack of study of the gospel and not believing fully in the teachings of the church has made you an easy target for the evil forces that are at the house. I think they are attracted to you and Chris. You are in spiritual danger."

"You're saying that all the paranormal activity is my fault! How can you say that? I didn't ask for this nor was I seeking out anything like this. The only interest in ghosts I've ever had is watching them on TV. Haven't you seen how hard all of this has been on me and Chris. How dare you judge me? What gives you the right?" I was livid with anger.

"I don't believe in those shows. I know what I know from my own experience and this is not the way to the truth. I think you've lost your way," Bob said calmly.

"Spare me the sanctimonious sermon," I said. "I can't live my life your way. Afraid to question something that doesn't fit within your neat set of rules. Does that make me an evil person?"

"I'm not saying you're a bad person, Anita. You're a beautiful woman and I know we had fun going out," he said. "But my conversion experience to my faith is true and I know you don't share that conviction."

"What I don't understand is that you've been dating me for sixteen months and you know I've been honest with you and have never tried to hide my spiritual beliefs. I can't be as committed to the faith as you. Why did it take you this long to tell me how you feel?" I asked.

"I was hoping you'd come around to my way of thinking," he said.

"Sorry to have disappointed you."

"Anita, we are two good people who are too different for this to work in the future."

I knew this was true. He wasn't saying anything I hadn't thought before. Maybe this was for the best. I don't think I could have ever been happy with him.

"I think you're right, Bob. I want to thank you for all your help at the house." I meant what I was saying.

"This doesn't have to be good bye, Anita, I'll see you again," Bob said.

"No, this is goodbye for good, Bob. Take care." I hung up the phone.

"What a mook, Mom," Chris said, after listening to part of the conversation. "I think the guy has a screw loose." He came over and gave me a hug.

I wiped a tear from my eye. "I think I've just been dumped over a ghost," I said.

"I guess there's always a first for everything," Chris said and smiled.

—⚏—

"He doesn't deserve you," my girlfriend Ellen said. "You know it's for the best."

I was sitting at the table at our favorite tearoom watching her pour Rose Hip tea into a pretty porcelain teacup. She had called me with a surprise invitation for a light lunch. Ellen and I had a psychic-like link that dated back to the eighth grade and we always sensed when something was wrong in each other's lives. I was grateful to have her advice and company that day. I hadn't had too many pleasant distractions since the whole situation with Paul's estate began and now this mess with Bob.

"I still don't know how anyone could date you for so many months and just drop you. He's like some kind of robot," Ellen said. "I think he has some unresolved intimacy issues."

"That's what my mother said too. I can't figure him out, Ellen. He seems to have a blind spot about his beliefs being the right one, and if you don't agree with his convictions, you're not good enough," I said.

"I was afraid when you started dating him again that this would happen. You've known each other almost twenty years and he thinks he can change you?" Ellen almost laughed.

"I know. I was hoping that by this time he had mellowed a bit, but I was wrong," I took a sip of my Chamomile tea. "I think we were both under the same illusion."

"You're an artist, Anita. You're a smart, creative person. Bob's a good person but with such a narrow outlook. You're an independent thinker. He's afraid to question outside his comfort zone and he's dismissing his experience at Paul's house. It was a recipe for disaster."

I sighed. "You're right, Ellen."

"You and I have talked about this before, Anita. We're interested in so many different things - religion, cultures and customs - that being devoted to one religion is so one note. That's not us.

"That sounds like something Paul would say."

"I don't know why all these things have happened to you at Paul's house, but you know I believe you. Right?"

"Of course I do, Ellen."

"I think Bob was afraid that you had tapped into something with Paul that challenged his belief system and couldn't explain away in any of his religious books or studies. He's scared."

"I made a call to a paranormal investigative group and they have to get back to me," I said. "I hope they can help. I can't thank you enough for your pep talk. You've been one of my best friends for what? Forty-five years."

"You're making us sound ancient. Here, let me drown your sorrows with some more tea." She poured more of the fragrant tea in my cup. "Sorry it's not something stronger."

"Maybe I'll sic my ghosts on him," I said. I gave her a wicked glance as I took a big bite out of my cucumber sandwich.

Ellen popped a piece of her scone into her mouth. "It would serve him right."

—m—

It was the second weekend in August when I received a surprise long distance call from a woman named Sylvia Goldberg. I never met her before but knew she was a good friend of Paul's. She had written a letter to Paul, which had been forwarded to me in July. Inside she had enclosed a group picture of Paul and his mother and Sylvia and her mother. The photo was dated September 2000 and had been taken on Sylvia's mother's 90th birthday.

She wanted to thank me for writing back and sending her the news about Paul. She was sorry to hear of his sudden death.

"It was so kind and thoughtful of you, Anita, to send me his prayer card and a copy of his obituary too," Sylvia said. "He was a good and devoted son to his mother, especially after his father died."

We chatted for a while and in our conversation Sylvia told me her mother had been a close friend and neighbor of the Jaegers for many years and that Mrs. Jaeger had been very upset when her mother had moved to Maryland to live with her.

"You mentioned in your letter that it's been some time since you were in touch with Paul. How long has it been, Sylvia?"

"It's been several years, but I was thinking about him this past Christmas and wanted to write for the longest time. Our families always spent time together at Christmas, sharing a meal and exchanging gifts. When I came across the picture, I wanted to send it to him. I'm sorry he never got it."

"I'm sorry too; it's a great picture of all of you. You said your mom was a close friend of Mrs. Jaeger?"

"Yes, Hilda and my mom were close friends, which was a bit unusual. We're Jewish and with the Jaegers coming from Germany after World War II, you would think it would have made an awkward relationship. Instead, they bonded over both being immigrants from Europe and the War, and since they both loved sewing and making clothes they became good friends," Sylvia continued. "Hilda Jaeger always contended her family and the German people never knew about what was happening to the Jews during the War. She claimed they were all ignorant of the facts of what happened to the Jewish people until much later when the horrors of the Holocaust came to light."

"Well you must have known how proud Paul was of his German heritage," I said. "He told me about his great-grandfather who received the Iron Cross and other medals in World War I, although he never volunteered much information about his father's involvement during the Second World War."

"Before we moved, Hilda came to visit my mother, knowing it could be the last time she would see her. She told her something she had kept to herself for many years. Hilda cried and confessed to my mother, that the German people *did* know all along what was happening to the Jews in Europe. She said she was so sorry about the lies and events that led to the Holocaust," Sylvia said. "I think she wanted to clear her conscience. She never saw my mother again and died the following year."

"I don't know what to say, Sylvia. I knew Paul for thirty years and he never let on about any of that. I wonder what else he had been keeping secret about his family all these years."

Then Sylvia told me something that made me almost drop the phone.

"Well you know, Anita, Mr. Jaeger *was* SS."

III.
PSYCHIC REPERCUSSIONS

"And I heard a voice from heaven saying unto me, Write: Blessed are the dead which die in the Lord from henceforth: Yea, saith the Spirit, that they may rest from their labours; for their works do follow them."
- Book of Revelation 14:13

Chapter 24

WHO YOU GONNA CALL?

"I can't believe that about Mr. Jaeger. Your suspicions about his military service could be right," I told my Dad one night when Chris and I were having dinner at my parents' house. "I knew him for fifteen years and he was always nice to me."

I knew Hans Jaeger as a short, slightly built man who worked for many years at a local hospital as a maintenance engineer. He was a talented carpenter who created furniture and novelty objects out of scrap wood.

"I told you. I thought he might be SS when I saw his military book," my dad said in a hoarse voice.

A slight chill went up my spine. I couldn't be sure he was an SS officer, based on what one person said, and knew it would take extensive research to find out if it was true. This was a terrible allegation, not one to take lightly, and it could be completely false.

I shuddered, remembering Paul telling me about his father's volatile temper and how he'd have to intervene during some of his parents' violent arguments. *We don't know what happens behind other peoples closed doors,* I thought.

Chris and I were sitting around the dinner table after putting in another long day of work at the house. My mother had made an almost full recovery from her nasty fall in May. She seemed to be her old self again, making spaghetti and meatballs for dinner and baking chocolate chip cookies for dessert. She was a force of nature.

"Do you think Paul knew about his father?" my mother asked.

"You know, Mom, I honestly don't know what he knew about his father. Paul once told me that his mother's family was from a small town in Germany and that they were active in the resistance against the Nazi Regime."

Chris leaned over and put his hand on his veteran grandfather's shoulder. "Mom, if you were in any branch of the German military, under Hitler, you'd be wearing some type of a Nazi uniform and fighting against someone like my Poppy."

"But Chris, he vaguely mentioned that his father had been in the Navy, but he never told me he served in World War II," I reiterated.

Just by the pictures we found of his father in uniform and that booklet Chris found under the carpet, I think Carl must have known his father was a Nazi.

"What did he say when you gave him all the family pictures?" Chris said.

"He never let on about any of it. He said his father was in a "special" military unit, and that he'd been selected from the Navy while the rest of the group was from other branches of the military," I said.

"Special, that's a good one," Chris said.

"These people had a lot of secrets, didn't they?" my mother asked.

"Nana, there's so much stuff we found out about Paul's family that had been kept secret for so long," Chris said. "It was all over the basement floor, stuffed in boxes under the bed, the closets, and in the garden house and the garage. They never threw out a thing, yet they're mad and haunting us for finding this all out. What were we supposed to do? Paul left Mom in charge, not his brother."

"No wonder Carl was upset about what I might find. I knew Paul and his family for thirty years, but it looks like I didn't know them at all," I said sadly, shaking my head.

"Did you have any activity today?" my dad asked, straining to get the words out.

"Yes, we did, dad. It started when we walked into the kitchen with the empty boxes. As we were bringing them I stacked them neatly in the corner, one on top of the other and when we brought in the last ones we saw that they had been thrown around as if some naughty little kid had a temper tantrum playing with his blocks."

"Later when we were in the mother's room, Mom saw a woman's lipstick pencil get thrown in her direction from the hallway," Chris said.

"That was when we came up from the basement after emptying the air conditioner's bucket into the sump pump drain and a magic marker was thrown into it. Then a slide hit me and the red knitting yarn was tossed into a container from where it had been sitting for the last several weeks. A wooden towel stick was thrown too. The items are always so random," I said and reached for a cookie.

"Did you tell them how I got hit in the face with a box of aluminum foil, Mom," Chris asked. "That hurt." Chris showed his grandmother the red mark on his forehead. "We smelled the damn cat again and then heard a "meow." I went to investigate and the tall upright sweeper fell over as if someone pushed it as I walked by."

"Anita, I'm worried about you and Chris going back there so many times. That place doesn't sound safe anymore," my mother said with deep concern in her voice.

"Nana, it's not Paul," Chris said. "He would never hurt us. There's something else there and it's a negative type spirit."

"That's all the more reason why you shouldn't go back. Did you ever call or get in touch with those ghost people?"

"Nana, you mean, 'who you gonna call ...Ghostbusters!'" Chris had always loved the movie *Ghostbusters* and got a kick out of being able to say the phrase with real purpose.

"They did get in touch with me, Mom. They're called E.R.I.E. Investigators, named after their founding members Eric, Regina, Ian and Elaine. That's clever, right? They're coming to Paul's house on August twenty-second around seven in the evening. They live about two hours outside of Philadelphia and they're bringing their medium with them," I said as I grabbed another cookie. "These cookies are really good, Mom."

"They'll have a long drive to get here," Chris said. "At least they're one group who's following through by coming to investigate. Mom tried contacting and e-mailing several groups she found on the internet. One famous group did respond but were too busy. This group got back to her right away. I hope they can help us. Maybe we'll finally get some answers."

"It's unbelievable, what's happening at his house," my mother said. "And to you missy, how much weight have you lost, Anita?"

"About seventeen pounds," I answered. "It's ok. I'm going to market it as The Paranormal Diet: Lose weight while you chase ghosts."

"And soon you'll lose so much weight you'll be invisible just like them," Chris said with a mischievous grin. We all laughed at the prospect of this new diet being on the market.

"Well, Nana at least you and Poppy believe us, not like some people," my son said referring to his aunt and uncle. They had made it clear they thought we were making things up, it must be our imaginations working overtime, or maybe Chris was doing it himself.

"The difference between my brother and me is that if he told me these things were happening to him, I would believe him without question. It really hurts to think that he can't give me the benefit of the doubt when he's never helped out at the house or spent any real time there. He knows I'm not the type of person to make this stuff up." I could feel my blood pressure rising. "Even accusing Chris, saying he's the real poltergeist. Sure, my son loves to throw heavy objects at his face so he can injure himself. Give me a break!"

"Don't get upset mom. It's not worth it."

I decided to change gears.

"Hey listen to this. It's a recording I got when I set this up in the living room when Kent helped us that Saturday."

I pulled out the mini tape recorder from my bag slung over my chair. I took out the tape from that particular day and put it into the recorder. I had written down the number when I heard this unusual sentence spoken so I could reference it quickly. "You'll hear Kent's voice and me talking about some audio tapes I had found that came from Germany. Listen closely and you'll hear another voice talking over us."

My parents got close to the recorder and I played that section of the tape.

> Me: *"Kent, these tapes have Paul's German relatives send-ing greetings to his parents, Hans and Hilda Jaeger. I'm keeping them for his brother."*
> Kent: *"That's good. I'm sure the brother will be grateful."*
> *I have to talk to you.*
> Me: *"Well, they should go to him."*

We never heard the strange voice audibly at the time.
I played it back several time for my parents on the highest volume.
I have to talk to you.
"Whose voice is that?" my mother asked.
Chris ventured a guess. "Sounds like Paul," he said.
"It *is* Paul," I told them. "I think he's desperate to get in touch with me."
My parents didn't know what to say. Their anxious faces said it all.
"E.R.I.E can't come fast enough, as far as I'm concerned," I said
"Who knows what they'll discover." Chris said. "You'll see, Mom, one day we'll be vindicated. People will realize that it's all true. Ghosts do exist."

Chapter 25

TRIPPED UP

It was August 18 and the E.R.I.E. Investigators were coming in a few days. Chris and I needed to focus on clearing out the enclosed porch that had been neglected up to this point. The realtor, Stan, had gotten back to us with a tentative offer, and that was great, but we had unfinished business with our ghosts. We needed to get as much evidence as possible for the remaining time we had at the house, so Chris set up his camcorder for the day.

I was in the living room on the phone, talking with my mother, once again preparing to clean. The work never seemed to end; no sooner would we have the living room cleared than it would fill up with stuff we brought from other rooms.

Swish!

"Chris, come over here. A pillow just flew across the room."

Chris came into the room. "Where did that come from?"

"It's one of the pillows that are always on the side chairs." I spoke into the phone. "Mom, I have to go, we have activity going on here."

"Oh, my God, be careful, Anita," my mother said.

"I hung up the phone and started to tense up, *I've got so much to do and they're starting in already,*" I said to myself as I headed back to the porch area. I hoped I could concentrate on what had to be done next.

Chris was filming in the mother's bedroom. There were still multiple items on one of the twin beds in the room and dozens of hatboxes from the closet were stacked on top of the wardrobe chest, awaiting Carl and his wife to inspect and pick up.

"A box of tissues just flew across the room," Chris called to me.

I came into the bedroom. Chris pointed to a full box of facial tissues that had flown off the headboard of the mother's bed and hit the wall across the room from where he was standing. I could see the dusty outline where the box had been sitting only moments earlier.

"My camera just went all blurry," Chris said, "This is the first time we've had any activity in the mother's room, isn't it, Mom?"

"Right, this seemed to be the last hold out for poltergeist activity. It's interesting."

Chris's cell phone rang. It was Kent. "Come on over now, there's stuff going on," he told his boss. He finished his call and turned to me. "He's stopping over with Ben. He has the van until tomorrow so he's taking the Rubber and Ficus trees."

"Great," I said. "I can finally clear that area of the living room with those big plants gone."

One of the hatboxes suddenly jumped off the wardrobe closet and hit the floor.

Chris was excited. "I got all that on tape, mom. I'll stay here a while longer and see what else I captured."

I walked into the hallway and as I went by the cat room, a wicker basket flew out the door. "Thanks I can use this." I picked it up and took it with me and as I reached the living room something hit my leg. "Hey, what the...?"

"What's going on, Mom?"

"Remember that small antique carpenter's level that you found in the cat room? It just hit me in the leg."

Chris turned the camera in my direction and something else flew in his view from the cat room. He picked it up and it turned out to be a record album, which he showed to me. Chris laughed. "It's, *Mother Angelica and her Nuns Sing for You.*" We both laughed at the crazy, random items thrown.

Chris turned around and headed back to the mother's room. When he stepped through the threshold, he yelled. "Something just tried to trip me!"

"What?" I came running.

"Something or someone just grabbed my leg and I almost tripped. What the fuck, man?"

I didn't like the sound of that. Were the spirits revving up for something?

"Are you ok now? Let me finish what I'm doing Chris."

I felt frantic. I was trying to stay focused but unseen forces were constantly distracting me. I walked back into the living room and a book sailing out of nowhere hit the floor. Poltergeist activity was happening every few minutes now.

"Where did that come from?" Chris called from the bedroom.

I picked up the book, *The Plumber out of the Sea*. "I think this was in the cat room. Is this supposed to be some kind of a message?" I asked, holding the book to the invisible forces. "I mean, really?"

I went back to the porch and started to pack up some small porcelain and metal knick-knacks from a tiered table. It looked like they had been sitting on the shelves for years; there were multiple layers of dust on them. I picked up a small female figurine and it started to jingle when the porcelain clapper hit the insides of the figurine's dress. I rang the bell for fun.

"Hey, Chris, remember? Every time a bell rings an angel gets its wings." That was my favorite line from the movie, *It's a Wonderful Life*

I then heard a door slam and Chris let out a long, surprised yell.

"Chris, Chris. What happened?" I screamed and ran to the bedroom and tried to open the door. The doorknob was stuck! I didn't know what had happened to my son or what horror I would find. I kept pulling and finally, I could open the door.

Chris was huddled in a far end corner of the bedroom. He could barely speak he was so frightened. He was laughing and crying at the same time, and it took him several minutes to compose himself.

"The fucking door slammed in my face! I was standing near it to hear what you were saying. You said something about an angel getting its wings and the door slammed in my face and I fell backwards."

"Oh my God, Chris, are you all right?"

He slowly got up from the floor and checked his camera. "I don't know if I got it on tape." A few seconds went by as he adjusted his camera and played it.

"An angel getting its wings"... it wasn't me saying that but an unfamiliar voice was heard on the tape. Then a hard slam and Chris' yell. *"The fucking door...."* Someone or something was mimicking Chris' voice. My blood ran cold.

Leaving a still shaken Chris, I walked back to the porch. We had to be extremely careful and on alert now. Our cleaning was making something very agitated. While I continued to pack the small knick-knacks in a box, a pillow from another chair got tossed at me. *What's with the pillows today?* I thought.

Chris stayed in the hallway and took the camera near the mother's room. He didn't go in but panned across the room. In view was the nightstand that had a small bag on it. In it were a bunch of new and used padlocks in different sizes and their keys that I had gathered. I still found it hard to believe one family would have so many.

"All the activity seems to be in the mother's room today," he said into the camera, as he turned away. He had taken only a few steps down the hallway towards me when we heard a loud crash from behind him. It was the same bag of locks that had been on the nightstand, now on the hall floor behind him.

I ran to pick them up to show them to the camera. "They're heavy," I said. "I bet they weigh a few pounds."

Chris shook his head. "It's incredible that they can lift something like that," he said.

"I know. That's what's so scary. They tossed it like it was nothing." I walked back to the porch. *Stay focused, Anita,* I said to myself, *you still have so much to do.*

I walked onto the porch and an electrical plug smacked against the doorframe.

"Knock it off," I yelled. "You spirits have too much time on your hands. Get an afterlife!"

As soon as I rolled a green hassock across the living room to get it out of the way, a slide hit me. "Real funny," I said.

"Chris, please come here and help me," I handed him some boxes from the porch. "Take these and put them over there for the Purple Heart." As he took them from me, the Hoover upright sweeper that was standing in the corner of the porch fell over.

"Jesus, that was right next to me," Chris said. "I'll get the camera and start filming here." He picked up the sweeper. He stood on the porch and caught his reflection in the mirror as he suddenly heard what sounded like a shaking rattle. When he turned around, he saw a fabric draft blocker, shaped like a snake and filled with pellets, was in the middle of the room.

"Mom, look, that yellow snaky dude just got tossed."

"Another paint brush got tossed over here," I said as I walked from the living room. "This is crazy today. Kent is missing all the fun."

A rolled up poster flew over us and I put it back with the others. Then, Chris followed me into the living room.

"Look at this junk," I lamented. "How am I going to get done in time before we sell the house? Ooooooo!" I wanted to tear my hair out I was so mad.

"Mom, I'll put the camera down for a while and help you. I feel bad that I'm not lending you a hand."

"You've been documenting the poltergeist activity and that's important. Besides, I'm not good with the camera," I sighed. "I don't know why everything is getting to me now. It's not like we haven't been through this ghostly stuff before."

"It's like you have battle fatigue, Mom. You can't blame yourself - it's all been too much. These aren't normal working conditions with these psycho ghosts. I'd like to know who else would do this."

After Chris finished his sentence, a boxed full-length mirror that was leaning against the wall flopped down in front of us. Chris started to laugh hysterically.

"Jesus, Paul, you're going to give me a heart attack," I called out to him.

"Good thing it didn't break, Mom. We don't need seven years bad luck."

—◦◦◦—

"I thought you said that Kent and Ben were on their way?" I asked Chris when we took a break. "You talked to him over an hour ago."

"Maybe he had another stop to make before he came here," Chris said. "You take it easy for a few minutes and I'll go back into the mother's room and ask some questions like they do on *Ghost Hunters*. It's an experiment. Why don't you do some EVP work with your tape recorder in the dining room?"

I looked at him cautiously. "Ok, but don't antagonize them, given your history in that room." I couldn't believe how brave my son was to go back into the bedroom.

Chris promised to be careful as he walked back to the mother's room.

He started his session.

"I'm here in Mrs. Jaeger's bedroom sitting on her bed. There's still a lot of stuff piled on the other bed," Chris said into the recorder on his camera. The room was now silent after so much activity had gone on during the last few hours.

"We are here to help you. Paul? Mrs. Jaeger? What was that? I thought I heard something. Sounded like a '*no*'. All the stuff that's happening here today is interesting." Chris cleared his throat. His allergies were really acting up with all the dust in the room.

"Please communicate with us." Chris panned across the room. "Let us know you're here."

Silence filled the room.

"I will ask a series of questions and try to let me know if you hear me. Are you upset that we're cleaning out the house?" Chris strained to hear. "I think I just heard something like a tap back here." Chris walked to the back of the bedroom and the furthest wall. He didn't know it while he was asking the questions that he had indeed recorded taps, as possible responses, on his camcorder. He didn't hear them in real time, but he heard them later when reviewing the tape.

"Is there more than one spirit here with us?"

A rapid series of taps followed.

"Are you trapped here?"

More taps followed.

"Are you evil or demonic in origin?"

The taps that followed were faint.

"Well, ok, I'm done asking. Thank you."

If Chris *had* heard the responses to his questions, he might not have calmly walked out of the room. Before he did, he placed a piece of folded red fabric on Mrs. Jaeger's bed, hoping that something would happen to it after he left the room. *After all, it is red,* he thought. He walked into the cat room where I was packing more boxes to take out to the living room.

"Whoops! Something just went between my legs."

"You're scaring me, Chris."

"It felt like a cat rubbing against my legs. What a weird sensation."

"Weird, that's the operable word here," I said sarcastically.

Chris went back into the mother's room and walked around the beds. The red cloth was still in the same position he had left it in.

He turned towards a noise he heard, and then looked into the mirror with his camera. He couldn't believe his eyes. The red cloth moved to the other twin bed.

I'll be damned. That was quick, he thought.

I pointed to some boxes. "Chris, put the camera down and take these from me."

Chris put the camera in the living room and helped me with the boxes from the cat room. "I thought we were finished in here," he said

"We're getting there," I said. "The rest of the junk on the bed will be gone by the end of the day. It's the overflow from emptying the cabinets in here. I only took about a hundred scarves from one of the cabinets. I keep marveling at the amount of accessories Paul's mother collected."

"Hoarding is the word, Mom."

When Chris walked down the hallway, another book flew by, hit the ceiling and bounced onto the floor. "That landed in the middle of the living room floor," he said.

Then, we heard a loud crash.

"It's the room divider," I yelled, and walked out of the cat room. It had fallen over to the opposite wall. "Look, Chris, it hit with such force it broke off the knob to the dimmer switch." Only the metal screw sticking out of the wall plate was left.

"Don't worry, it screwed back on," Chris said. "They're really messing with us today. Where the heck is Kent?"

"When he comes, would you please have him help you carry that room divider out of here. That thing is dangerous." By that point, I was very nervous, but I felt a little relieved when I heard Kent's voice in the distance.

"Is it safe to come in?" Kent called as he made his way through the kitchen with Ben, his new employee. "Sorry we're late guys, but we had to make another stop. What's been going on?"

Chris brought them up to date.

Ben seemed a bit skeptical when he heard us talk about the latest ghostly activity. "Kent told me about his experiences here with you at the house. I don't know if I believe all that stuff."

Ben was a 6'4" husky ex-marine who Kent had hired recently as his new Manager of Sales. He was a likeable guy, if not a bit overbearing.

"Well, Ben, if you stay for a while you may change your mind," I said, "Say 'hi' to the camera. Chris is filming all this."

All of a sudden, Kent jumped with a surprised look on his face and put his hand on the back of his neck. "Something just touched me. Is there a bug or something on my neck?" he asked Ben who was standing right next to him.

Ben looked at the back of Kent's shirt. "I don't see anything."

I looked at Ben and wondered if I'd just seen a slight look of trepidation on his face.

"Take a look around, Ben, it's not every day you visit a haunted house," I said, laying it on thick. "Maybe you'll get touched like my cousin did when she was here."

"Touched by an angel? I hope. That *was* weird," Kent said, still looking around for the invisible bug.

I laughed. "Did you forget where you are, Kent?"

Smack! Something hit me on the shoulder.

"What was that?" Ben was almost speechless.

I picked up a pin with a guardian angel design on it and showed it to them.

"That came from the direction of the mother's bedroom, Mom," Chris said.

"You better wear it, Anita. I think someone is trying to tell you something," Kent said incredulously as I pinned it to my shirt collar.

"You're the one who mentioned angels, Kent," I said.

Ben looked nervous and stepped a little close to the kitchen. I think he was ready to make a break for it.

"We can't stay too long," Kent said. "Let's get the plants. Thanks again, Anita, they will look good in the lobby. You sure it's ok to take them? Does anyone else want them?"

"They're all yours. I would have asked the neighbor next door, but the whack-a-do really ticked me off," I said.

Kent laughed at my nickname for Paul's next-door neighbor. "What happened?"

"Tell him, Mom."

"I was out near the garden house and she came over and had the nerve to ask me if she could dig up some of Paul's daffodil bulbs in the front yard," I said.

Kent couldn't stop laughing. "What did you say?"

"I said *no*. I told her she'd have to buy her own. I said that if I see any holes in the front yard that I'd come after her for trespassing! Poor Paul didn't spend all that time planting those five hundred daffodils bulbs in his garden to have some nut-job dig them up. He had some bizarre neighbors and I understand why he kept to himself. They're such vultures!"

Chris, Kent and Ben were all laughing. "You're too much, Anita," Kent said.

They finally settled down and Kent and Ben started to carry the trees out the side door to the van. When they passed the small statue of Jesus that was on the counter top near the door, the statue did a "fly by" into the dining room. Kent and Chris really lost it after that.

"Isn't that the same statue that flew up from the basement when I was here?" Kent asked Chris. By this time, they were laughing hysterically.

"I guess they don't want the plants to move out," I said.

"Kent, does that mean we'll have haunted plants in the lobby?" Ben asked with a serious look on his face

Kent hesitated for a moment.

"Don't listen to him, Kent. Take Jesus with you. He'll protect you." I turned and looked at my son with a wide roll of my eyes.

"God, I hope so." I heard Chris mutter under his breath.

Kent and Bill were treated to one more trick the ghosts had up their sleeves. When they came back into the living room to say goodbye, they heard a noise.

"What was that?" Ben asked, concerned.

I went to investigate and discovered the dimmer knob was missing from the hallway light switch. "Not again, we already had problems with this knob."

I told Kent and Ben what had happened with the room divider, which reminded me to ask them to take it out to the garage.

"Thanks for doing that, guys," I said.

"Did you find the knob to the light switch yet?" Kent asked me when he came back in the house.

"No, *they're* playing with it. This is something new. If I have to spend all day looking for it, Mr. Paul, I'm going to be really mad at you. Give it back!" I said to my deceased friend.

Ben was slightly bewildered. "Who's she talking to?" he asked Kent in a low voice.

"It's her dead friend, Paul. This was his house," Kent said.

Ben must have thought I was crazy. Who could blame him?

A few seconds later, a loud smack came from the mother's bedroom.

"You have to be kidding me," I ran into the mother's room and saw what had hit the wall lying on the carpet. Everyone was right behind me.

"The knob, it's the knob." I showed it to them."

They were all shocked. "No way! Are you serious?"

"That's incredible, Anita. He heard you," Kent said.

"I know. He seems to hear everything," I turned to Ben. "Is seeing believing? How about taking a tour of the basement?"

"No thanks. I've seen way too many horror movies to know you don't go in the basement."

As Ben made his way out the kitchen door, the red fish comb came from the direction of the cat room and flew near Kent. He recognized what it was and beat a hasty retreat to the door too.

"It's time to go!

—m—

We were glad that we had the visit from Kent and Ben because, once again, it reinforced the idea that we weren't the only ones seeing and experiencing the inexplicable events going on in the house

No sooner had they left than things were thrown in the living room and kitchen. I moved the camera so that it was sitting on the dining room table facing the living room, but as soon as I moved the camera in one direction, the spirits would do something else in the opposite direction. About a half hour went by and we recorded numerous items being thrown as we continued to work, including a spoon that hit a box in the kitchen. The poltergeist activity was a constant distraction, made worse by the heat and humidity that not even the air conditioner alleviated.

My nerves were stretched so tight that I thought they'd snap any minute. I'd had enough. "Chris, would you please stop dumping junk on the table. Look at this mess!"

"What do you want me to do?" he asked.

"Either pack it for donations or throw it out. That's the third time I've found that angel in a different spot. Stop moving it around. You are making double work for me."

"I'm not doing that!" he raised his voice. "*They* keep taking stuff out of the boxes and trash!"

"Ok, I'm sorry, but I want you to stop wandering around looking for the junk they are throwing. You are wasting so much time. I want to get the rest of this stuff packed up and get out of here. It's so hot!" I took the wandering angel and packed it away.

Ping!

A plastic bottle hit the bag of keys and locks that I was going to give Carl. They were on the desk in the living room. He was coming on Saturday morning to take a load of boxes that I had stacked in the living room for him.

"It's an old bottle of sunscreen. Where did it come from?" I said to Chris and the camera.

"From hell," he said, trying to make a joke. "They probably need... like SPF one million."

I laughed nervously. Were the ghosts hearing all of this?

Bang! A roll of scotch tape hit the glass breakfront.

I guess they were, I thought.

Smack! A packet of erasers flew behind the credenza.

"Stop it," I yelled. "Leave us alone."

Chris grabbed the camera and pointed it at the kitchen doorway. He had limited range since we had forgotten to bring the long extension cord and the batteries had drained within the first hour we were in the house.

Crash!

"What was that?" Chris asked, and then walked past me to investigate. I grabbed the camera and panned over to the back hallway where we had heard the sound. Within a split second, I heard a loud sickening thud. Chris yelled out and I turned around and saw him flat on the floor.

"Oh my God! Christopher, are you all right?" I screamed.

He didn't answer me. He was sprawled face down in the middle of the living room floor.

I heard a muffled voice coming from the carpet. "Ouch! Those bastards."

"Chris, what happened? Did you trip over the green hassock?"

"No. Ow... my wrist, my chin." He lay still on the floor and could hardly talk.

"What was it?" I asked.

"I don't know...something grabbed me."

He still wasn't moving or getting up. I rushed to his side and sat down next to him. "Honey, did you break your wrist? Please, answer me." I was frantic and terrified. How badly hurt was my son?

"Those fucking bastards. I hurt my knee."

"Can you get up? I'll take you to the hospital."

"I think I broke my watch. Where are my glasses?' Chris got up slowly to a sitting position and found his glasses. They weren't broken. "Ow...my wrist."

"What happened?" I asked again. "You were next to me and the next second you were on the ground."

"I was walking by the hassock to see what was going on back there and I felt someone grab my leg or ankle and I lost my balance. It happened so fast I couldn't catch myself and I landed hard on my knee and wrist." He was rocking back and forth to ease the pain. "You son of a bitch!"

I quickly ran into the kitchen for cold water and an ice pack.

"Here, put this on your hand," I said. I was furious that something had attacked my son. "You no-good cowards!" I yelled. "Show yourselves. How dare you attack my son! That's too bad you don't want us to move your God damn crap!"

Chris was red in the face, still trying to calm down from his confrontation with the supernatural. "It's not them, Mom, it's not the Jaegers."

"We don't know that for sure."

"Something's been trying to trip me up all day. First, it felt like a cat between my legs, then near the mother's room and now this. It's something else, some kind of evil presence. It got you outside the Garden House."

"I'm done. I didn't sign up for this. To hell with this place!"

Chris looked around the room and wiped his face with a towel. "Look at all we still have to do. We must have another two months of work here, it never ends." He pointed to all the boxes.

He and I were both near tears. It was a pathetic sight.

"Do you want to quit?" I asked. "I'll call the lawyer and tell him that after Carl picks up the family boxes, he can come in here and finish. Let him get thrown to the ground!"

After moving his wrist back and forth, Chris began to feel a little better; we knew it wasn't broken. He didn't want to go to the hospital and just wanted to finish up and get the hell out.

Things seemed to quiet down suddenly so we finished clearing the living room for the investigators as best we could. I didn't want anyone else to get hurt. We finally checked out the back hall. Large amounts of photo slides were spilled out from a box and all over the floor.

"Look, Mom, it's a box of colored slides from Colonial Williamsburg."

Damn it, Paul. What are you trying to tell me?

We knew we had a decision to make if we wanted to continue working under what had become very dangerous circumstances. We decided to hold out for the investigators who were coming on Saturday night and help us find out what we were dealing with. Would these people be the ones to give us the much-needed answers?

Chapter 26

GHOSTS IN THE MIDST

It was beginning to rain hard as Chris and I made our way to Paul's house. Chris looked at his watch. "Not bad, it's only 6:15," he said. "What time are the investigators supposed to meet us there?"

"They said they would try to be there by 7:00 but I don't know if this rain is going to hold them up. They have a long drive," I said with a sigh, already tired before the evening began. This was the second time I'd been at Paul's house that day since I had met Carl there at 9:30 AM so he could pick up the load of boxes I had packed for him. After he left, I stayed at the house to clean up the bathroom and straighten up the living room. I didn't get home until after 1:00 PM. Chris had worked with Kent all day and didn't get home until 5:00 PM, then quickly showered, ate dinner and packed his camcorder with a fresh tape. He was going to film the investigation, which turned out to be a wise decision.

We pulled up to the house and turned off the alarm. I wondered if the spirits knew who was coming and if they were going to show themselves. We entered the living room and Chris couldn't get over how much more room there was, now that Carl had taken the boxes, desk and other items with him.

"Wow, Mom, it looks good. There's plenty of room for them to set up their cameras and equipment."

I looked at my watch and it was past seven. My cell phone rang and it was Regina, one of the members of the E.R.I.E. investigation team.

"Hi, Anita, we are on our way but the traffic is terrible. We probably won't be there until 8:00 or later," Regina said. "It's raining buckets and traffic is at a crawl."

"We know it's bad out there so just drive safely," I said. "If you need better directions as you're approaching off the main highway, give us a call."

"Thanks, Anita, we'll be there as soon as we can."

"What's up, Mom? They're still coming, aren't they?"

"Yes, but the rain is holding them up. They won't be here for at least another hour so we might as well get comfortable. Let's put on all the lights—this place is too damn dark and creepy at night.

———

Chris started to doze off in a chair and I sat on the sofa thinking of how far we had progressed with the house. With the sound of heavy rain hitting the roof, I realized it was the first time I had sat on the sofa relaxing. For a moment, I remembered the first time I had sat in the Jaeger's living room with Paul, drinking coffee and eating a delicious homemade German dessert with his mother and father. My silent reverie was broken when a small box was tossed from the hallway onto the living room floor, spilling its contents.

Chris was startled out of his sleep. "What the...?" he asked.

"Here we go, they're starting up," I said.

"Can't they let a guy take a rest," Chris said. He went into the kitchen for a bottle of water and I followed to do the same.

He opened the refrigerator door and something came right at him.

"Ouch! Hey!" he yelled.

"What the hell was that?" I asked.

Chris rubbed his nose, bent down and picked up something small and pink. "I just got hit in the face with this." He held up a small summer sausage.

I laughed. "Are you kidding?" It was funny. "I'm sorry I laughed, Chris, but what these ghosts keeping coming up with is ridiculous."

Chris started to laugh too. "I know. Where did this come from? I saw you clean out the refrigerator myself."

Then, we heard several thuds.

We both went into the living room and saw that several pillows were thrown into the hallway.

"Hope they perform for these people like they just did for us," Chris said.

It was 8:45 P.M when the investigators finally arrived. The unrelenting rain continued to come down in sheets as the team entered the kitchen.

Eric and Regina were a husband and wife team whom I had spoken with on the telephone and they introduced Elaine, their medium friend who worked with them only on the more interesting cases. Ian, the other member of the team, was unable to make it. They told us how fortunate we were that Elaine was available for our investigation, as she was considered one of the top mediums working in the paranormal field.

"Thanks so much for coming on a night like this. We really appreciate it," I said.

"That's what we do—have ghosts will travel," Eric said. He was tall and slender with dark hair and a mustache. "Where's a good place to set up?"

I showed them the living room. They set down their large heavy black boxes of equipment and got right to work. It felt like we were in a TV episode of one of those paranormal shows. Each one of the members was wearing a black shirt and cap with a ghost logo on it. They took out hand-held digital cameras and voice recorders to capture EVPs and another small instrument that looked like an EMF detector, a meter that measures low-level electromagnetic fields. On one of the paranormal TV shows Chris and I watched, we learned that there was a theory in ghost hunting that paranormal activity or spirits can cause a higher than average reading of electromagnetic energy within an otherwise normal environment. The team was anxious to get started after I described some of the activity we'd experienced in the house and what we had just encountered before they arrived. Chris showed Eric around the house and he proceeded to record base readings on his meter.

"We'd like to get an initial sweep of the house and the rooms to see what areas are the most active before we set up anything else," Eric said.

Regina and Elaine followed me into Paul's bedroom. Regina was petite and blonde and Elaine was taller with short brown hair. Immediately, Elaine said that she felt a presence in the dark room and that it was my friend, Paul.

"He's earthbound," she said as she walked around his bed. "He's upset. He wants to know what happened to all his stuff. I feel heaviness in the legs. There is pressure in the chest too." Elaine continued to walk around the dark bedroom. "He is rubbing his leg and having a hard time lifting it... and he's having trouble getting his breath."

This was incredible to hear since I hadn't told her about his health problems. All I had told Regina and Eric on the phone was that I had a friend who lived alone in his house and that he had passed away suddenly. I hadn't told them the cause of his death.

"I get the feeling that he was sick before he died, but he wasn't aware of how sick he really was," Elaine continued.

"Yes, you're right, Elaine, he had asthma for years and had injured his leg early last spring, but he didn't go to the doctor for it," I said. "I was worried about him, but he just brushed it off.

"Paul, can you let us know you are here? Can you move something? Knock for us?" Elaine asked calmly. "I'm here to help you."

Regina continued to snap pictures around the room while Elaine tried to establish further contact with Paul.

"Make a noise for us, Paul?" Regina asked.

"He said, 'I'm not doing this on cue,'" Elaine repeated, apparently annoying Paul's spirit.

Chris had his camcorder on and he came to where I was standing by the doorway. We peered into the dark bedroom, not entering, trying to avoid distracting the investigators.

"How many spirits do you think are here, Elaine?" Eric asked, holding his meter near the doorway.

"Seven," she answered with certainty.

"Seven?" Regina echoed.

"Seven? Wow, it seems we have a full house," I said as I turned to Chris who was just as surprised as I was. "No wonder there's been so much activity."

"Paul, can you say something on my recorder?" Regina asked. "We are only here to help you. You can talk into my red light."

Help!

"Guys, did you get that?" Chris asked.

They hadn't heard it or picked it up on their recorders. But we had.

"The air is thick...very thick. It's choking me, like my throat is tightening up and it's right here over his bed," Elaine said, rubbing her throat.

"He's projecting how he was feeling onto you Elaine," Regina said. "Anything you want to tell us, Paul?"

"He's resisting. He's telling me that he doesn't believe in us and who we are and what we're doing here." Elaine shook her head. "He keeps going on and on about this." She suddenly turned and pointed to Chris. "You're an easy target. They love messing with you."

"I know. I'm the one who just got hit in the face with a sausage."

"That's his way of communicating," Elaine said.

"Tell him to use cotton balls next time, same result," Chris said sarcastically.

She walked around the bedroom again. "Are you still here, Paul?"

We all heard a knock.

We stood silently, hanging on every word.

Elaine spoke. "He's definitely earthbound, but he's not angry. He just doesn't want to cross over. He's telling me there's really nothing there for him."

Hearing what Elaine said disturbed me. What did Paul mean *nothing there for him?*

"His mom... has crossed over—she's not here. She comes to visit and then goes. Other members of his family come in visitation also, but they don't stay. His dad's energy is still here, he hasn't crossed over. Paul's energy is here with his dad. They are both earthbound."

I was surprised hearing his father was still in the house and had a hard time processing all of this. Knowing Paul's history with his father, I wondered what had caused him to forego crossing into the eternal light and instead stay here, in a kind of limbo with his father.

"He doesn't like that you moved all his stuff," Elaine said.

"I'm sorry, Paul, but we had no choice but to clear out your room. You left me all your collectibles, and the rest of your stuff needed to be packed so we could sell the house. That's what you put in your will," I said, hoping he heard me.

Chris walked back to Eric, who was in the kitchen, doing a sweep with his detector.

"I got a very high reading here in the kitchen and the dining room. "It's around a five," he called to Regina.

"Ok," Regina said, as she and Elaine walked into the parents' bedroom.

"Did the father pass from a stroke? I'm getting from the father that his head hurts...it hurts, he's telling me," Elaine said.

"You're two for two, Elaine," I said. I was quite impressed with her ability as a medium. She seemed to be the real deal.

They made their way to the cat room and Chris and I explained to Elaine and Regina how much time it had taken to clear out the rooms. I showed them the red yarn, pens, combs and spools of thread that were recent projectiles. I told them Paul's mom had been an accomplished dressmaker and designed and made clothes.

"What was the mother's name, Anita?" Regina asked.

"Hilda."

I asked Elaine if the spirits had told her anything about the significance of throwing red objects.

"Red is easy to see, his mom wanted you to know that." Elaine said.

"Oh, wow, so it is her," I said. "We've definitely felt a feminine presence at times."

"The father keeps saying that his head hurts and that he is very con-nected to this house. He doesn't want to leave." Elaine stepped out of the cat room. "He is really attached to all this stuff."

"Elaine, is it going to be hard to cross someone over that doesn't want to go?" Regina asked in a whispered tone as they walked back into the living room.

"Hell, yes!" She answered empathically.

Elaine and Regina joined us in the living room and sat down on the sofa. Elaine moved to the edge of the cushion and seemed to be listen-ing intently to something beyond our hearing.

"The father is scared to cross over. They both are," she said resting her head in her hand.

"Both?" I asked.

"That's right, your friend and his father."

I didn't know what to say.

Things seemed very quiet in the house now. Eric came into the room and announced that they should go down into the basement, so they followed with me leading them down the steps.

"I'm getting around a seven or eight right here," Eric said as he took his EMF detector and walked around the room. He ruled out electric outlet interference and other wiring after he checked them and deter-mined they were giving out weak readings.

We showed them around the basement, pointing out where all the new construction of the sump pump had taken place, and where the pink hankie was still stuck in the ceiling rafters. They were intrigued with more stories of the many incidents of poltergeist activity we had down there while clearing out all the stuff.

The investigators began their sweep of the dimly lit basement and I told them, if they thought there was a lot of junk down here now, they should have seen it five months ago.

"Who threw that hankie up in the ceiling? That was pretty cool, Dude," Regina shouted into the air.

It was Eric's turn. "Who is down here, we thought we heard foot-steps down here when we were in the living room."

I feel you've got some kind of a mix of paranormal activity going on down here, Anita," Elaine said. She looked down at the floor. "It feels ... Native American? Something's attached to that." She walked over to the area near the sump pump. "When you had the basement fixed, it stirred things and opened up something here. All hell broke loose. Am I right?"

"That's about right," I said.

Elaine looked around the room. "You mentioned on the phone to Regina that Paul collected so much from around the world. Where's his stuff now?" She asked.

"Most of it has been stored and I have some of the more delicate, breakable items at my house," I said

"Hmm... that's not good. I'd get rid of them if I were you," she said.

"But it's not that simple," I said a bit frustrated. "I haven't had a chance to inventory all the items as I've been too busy here. I have no idea of their historical significance or monetary value. I can't just throw them out."

I wasn't sure I believed or was convinced what she was implying; was she saying that somehow the inanimate objects had some type of spirits associated with them? This could explain what happened to me in the garden house.

"Well, don't say I didn't warn you," Elaine replied.

"Are you picking up anything down here, Elaine?" Eric asked changing the subject.

"No, I'm not getting anything."

"They seem quiet tonight," Chris said. "Maybe they met their match."

We continued to walk around the basement while they took more pictures and used techniques to provoke a response. About ten minutes passed and Eric and Regina seemed bored, and even annoyed that there wasn't any real activity for them to witness.

"Is anyone down here? You can talk to us." Regina asked. "What's the family's nationality?"

"They're German," answered Chris.

"That's something we have in common, I'm one hundred percent German. Sprechen sie Deutsch?" Regina asked. "Come on, materialize!"

"I'm getting that cobwebs feeling around my legs," Chris said, "Are you guys feeling anything like that?" Maybe it just took them a while."

"Shh...I'm hearing footsteps above us," Elaine said. "Maybe we should go back upstairs."

"I'll chill down here for a while," Eric said as he pulled over a chair and sat down. "I'm only a few years younger than this fellow was. Maybe he'll relate to me better if it's just *me* down here."

"Brave man," Chris said laughing as the rest of us went back upstairs.

—⁂—

Elaine settled on the living room sofa as Regina sat down in a side chair. They accepted my offer of a cold drink and then I pulled out a dining room chair and sat near Chris who had set up his camcorder on the dining room table. It was over an hour into the investigation and I couldn't help wondering if they thought they were wasting their time. I got the impression that they had expected more "spirit" action by now and they didn't seem to be as enthusiastic as when they first arrived. I was getting nervous. Maybe I just didn't want these people to think we were making the whole thing up. Now I was hoping for some paranormal activity. *This is crazy,* I thought.

Regina asked me more questions about Paul's work and the circumstances surrounding his death and that of his parents. They genuinely seemed not to know any of this information, which convinced me they had entered this investigation without doing any research ahead of time.

I answered their questions and asked them if they would reveal anything to us that they had picked up so far on their recorders.

"We'll have to review the evidence when we get home and let you know then," Regina explained.

After several minutes, Elaine cleared her throat. "He was a peaceful and kind person." She was speaking of Paul. "There's no doubt in

189

my mind that he was an eccentric type and a hoarder. He didn't like strangers in the house and he was very attached to his possessions. In fact, he can't let go, which is weird, since he left you in charge to get rid of anything in the house. He's torn about that. That's the reason why he's still here."

"So what do we do?" I asked. "We still have to be here and finish with his estate. How do we continue working with the ghosts in the midst of all this?"

"We have at least another two months of work here. What are we supposed to do in the meantime?" Chris asked. "Can you please give us some advice?"

"I think if you clean, clear and bless this house, they'll move out. If it's just a shell, they have nothing to be attached to," Regina said. "I think that's the way to go."

What she said made sense, but it seemed too simplistic an answer. If only we could do just that and all would be normal, but something told me there was more going on in the house than they realized. There was a strange dynamic present that wasn't being addressed and I wasn't sure what it was. Had Elaine picked up on it?

"But Regina, they don't want the house cleared out. They're distracting them from finishing the house," Elaine said, pointing at us. "They know it's the end. I think this is a last ditch effort to stop them from emptying the house."

Clink.

"What was that?" Chris asked. He went into the kitchen, where the sound had come from, and came back with a key in his hand.

"This must have hit the basement door. It was on the floor," he said as it showed it to Regina and Elaine.

"Paul, did you just throw the key?" Regina asked.

"He's telling me he doesn't have to answer you or talk to me. He just said, *why do I have to talk to you?* He's being aloof and his father is arrogant," Elaine said, visibly insulted. "Like, who are you?"

The whole time Elaine was talking in the living room, Chris had been sitting at the dining room table with his camera focused on her. He heard a noise and turned his camera just in time to capture a flickering yellow light on the kitchen table.

"What was that?" he asked. "That's so strange.'

"Shh."

Meow

"Did you guys hear that?" he asked.

We all heard it.

"I smell something burning," Regina said. Suddenly alarmed, she got up from the chair.

"I don't smell anything," I said.

"I wish they made equipment that captures phantom smells," Regina said.

"Well something just interfered with my camera. I didn't pick up the last few minutes of our conversation," Elaine said, clearly annoyed. "They don't want us to record them."

"It's starting," Chris announced. "I have had several taps on my camera and I don't know where it's coming from."

Eric came back up the stairs from the basement with nothing to report.

"That's because it's all up here, dear," Regina said to her husband. "We better set up the tripods here in the living room if we're going to capture anything. There's a lot of activity all around this area."

Eric didn't say anything and just sat down on one of the side chair and didn't do what his wife asked. Chris turned to me and gave me a look that said, *isn't that why you're here tonight and brought all this special equipment?*

I was thinking the same thing. Eric seemed a bit nonchalant, but his team had only been there for two hours. He wasn't giving the spirits a chance. Chris and I had been coming to Paul's house almost five months before the constant poltergeist activity started.

Let's continue with an EVP session," Eric finally said. He adjusted his handheld device. "If you want to make contact with us, we are going to be here all night! If not, we'll just have to come back!"

"Paul, it's time for you and your father to move on. Your mother is waiting for you over there," Elaine said softly.

We waited for an answer.

Elaine replayed her recorder but there was nothing.

"My last EVP didn't record. Let me try this again." Elaine's eyes suddenly opened wide.

"He just told me abruptly, 'I'm not going without my father.'"

Elaine was clearly frustrated with Paul. "He's saying to me that if his father won't go then he won't go. He would cross over, but not without his father."

This was all so hard to believe because Paul and his father were never close in life. Paul always said to me, no matter what he did or achieved he could never measure up to his father's standards. Was he still trying to get his father's approval, even now in death?

Elaine squinted as if straining to pick up something else Paul was trying to tell her. "He's telling me he had a feeling his father was stuck here. That he would cross over but since his dad is stuck here, he's still attracted to stay here. There is something with a uniform that's related to the father."

My heart started beating fast hearing what Elaine had just said.

"I see the father as...," Elaine stopped in mid-sentence. She had her eyes closed as if fighting to get something out. "He's the one who pushed you, Chris. He was very hands-on, physically violent and aggressive, especially towards women. Part of it was his German traits. He was a controlling type person and very strict. He wasn't nice to his wife either. He was very harsh. He pushed you too, Anita, in the garden house."

Chris and I didn't know what to say. We were finally getting some answers to the perplexing questions about what we were dealing with. A complete stranger seemed to be prying into the Jaeger's innermost secrets. I was certain Elaine *was* making contact with them. The next thing she said riveted us all.

"His father is afraid to cross over. It's like he's saying, 'forget about it'. He is really scared what's over there, doesn't know what's waiting for him, that's why he doesn't want to cross over."

"So if the dad doesn't cross over, Paul won't cross over either? I asked.

Elaine continued. "Something about women and children are involved. I get the impression that he was commanded to do something... not very nice. He keeps saying that he had to carry out his orders. He was told to do this—it was not his choice. He had no free will in the matter."

She didn't say anything for several minutes. The atmosphere in the room became humid and clammy.

"Are you able to get anything else, Elaine? I don't want to influence you with certain information I have," I said

"No, go ahead, I'm stuck. Can you throw some light on all this?" she asked.

"Well we found some evidence that Mr. Jaeger was a Nazi, serving in the Navy during World War II," I said. "We have a photo of him in his uniform."

"Oh, now everything makes sense!" Elaine exclaimed. "The uniform and the fact that he keeps saying he had no choice and was just following *orders*."

"Is he afraid of facing judgment on the other side?" Regina asked.

"Yes, he's afraid. I'm also picking up that he had a really nasty, early life growing up and..."

Elaine never finished the sentence.

"My camera just died," Chris said.

Everyone's camera and equipment batteries were drained at the same time.

"Someone doesn't want us to record that," Chris said and got out his power cord. The team took out their extra battery packs too.

"What's that boom, boom, BOOM?' Elaine asked.

The sound came from the parent's room. Regina and Elaine looked startled. Then, Chris heard a smack and retrieved what turned out to be a silver thimble at the kitchen door. It was ice cold.

"Well, the mother was into sewing wasn't she?" stated Regina.

Eric held up his arms to silence everyone. "Shh, I hear something."

"I thought it sounded like a pipe hitting something," Chris said

Eric walked into the kitchen and stood at the top of the stairs, listening.

"I'm going downstairs to take some pictures," Eric said, but he didn't get far. "Ouch! What the...?"

Regina became alarmed when she heard her husband call out. "Eric, what is it?"

"I got hit in the back of the neck with a key."

She ran back into the kitchen. "Hey!" Regina's camera got hit with a bunch of paper clips. Chaos ensued as we all ran to the kitchen to see what was happening there. At first, Regina was startled, and then she started to laugh. We all started to talk at once as a Ping-Pong ball bounced all around the kitchen.

We got caught up in the fun of this unexpected show and Regina called out, "Good one, Paul, you're too funny!"

We settled in the living room. Eric sat on one of the overstuffed chairs and talked about what had just happened to him. It was apparent the investigators didn't seem to scare easily. They were having fun.

I pretended to rummage through some boxes to see if that would continue the activity.

Squeak, squeak

"I think it's coming from the basement," Chris said. "They may be trying to distract us."

We all walked to the top of the basement stairs. We heard someone walking around, and then people talking in whispers.

"Guess we should try and go down again," Eric said

We walked down to the basement as a group once again. Chris left the camera on the dining room table, as the power cord wasn't long enough to bring downstairs.

"I'll leave it on, Mom, and finish using up the tape," Chris said.

That was a good idea, because what he recorded was unexpected.

—⁓—

We stayed downstairs with Regina when, only 10 minutes later, Elaine and Eric went upstairs. Chris and I were getting the feeling that Eric wasn't very pleased with how the investigation was going; we soon learned we were correct.

They returned to the dining room and sat at the table where the camcorder was. They didn't know at the time that it was still turned on. It picked up Eric and Elaine's conversation that wasn't meant for our ears.

Eric stood by the table talking to Elaine in a low voice and questioned if Chris had somehow hit him on the back of his neck with the key. Elaine responded to Eric that would be hard to do since he had been in her line of sight from the living room the whole time.

Eric: *"I think that's all that's going to happen tonight."*

There was a noise and a shout from Regina about something being thrown down in the basement.

Elaine: *"Aww Geezz, we'll be down in a minute".*

Eric: *"I don't get it. I thought there would be more stuff happening."*

Elaine: *"What do you mean?"*

Eric: *"Well, like my sister's house...that's really active. They are planning to move out of the house".*

Elaine: *"Oh, really?"*

Eric: *"But here? Psst. When we talked on the phone with her, she mentioned all this activity. I thought we'd get a lot more than we're getting here tonight."*

Elaine: *"Well, you're a professional skeptic."*

Eric: *"After all the things she claimed happened, I'm like walking around and there's nothing. I want something more."*

Elaine: *"But Eric, it's not like there's nothing here, there is."*

Eric: *"Yeah, but not enough. We need more stuff to happen."*

Elaine: *"I don't think it's dangerous, it's just a lot of stuff the spirits are attached too and they are playing around."*

Eric: *"I think we are wasting our time. Like that investigation we are doing at that old state hospital with the child ghost...we may really have something there."*

Eric: *"Look Elaine, in back of you, I think the camera's on?"*

Elaine turned to look straight at the camera, just shrugged, and then laughed. *"So?"*

Meanwhile, unaware of what Eric and Elaine were discussing, we continued to walk around the basement with Regina. We mentioned Paul being a writer and how many newspapers we sorted through had different articles he had written for them. Just as we turned a corner, a red tipped felt pen flew in front of her and landed on the floor. Several other bangs followed as Regina screamed and then flew up the stairs to get Eric. We heard her yell excitedly at Eric and Elaine as we waited at the bottom of the steps.

"What are you two doing? Get your butts down here, you're missing everything. A red pen just hit the f'n floor. There's all kinds of stuff happening! There was a small light bulb that was tossed and bouncing on the floor!"

"Ok, ok" Eric said and reluctantly Elaine got up, too.

Smack!

Another key hit the steps as they made their way down to the basement, but nothing else happened after they arrived. After a short time, we all went back to the living room where our guests placed themselves on the side chairs and sofa. I sat down opposite Chris at the dining room table. He was clearly concerned about the lack of enthusiasm Eric and Elaine were exhibiting. No tripods were set up and nothing else came out of their black suitcases. This was not the investigation they had originally promised us.

They started to shout out questions again, trying to provoke responses.

"Do something to let us know you're here," Eric commanded. "Why don't you knock over my chair? Why don't you turn the lights on and off?"

Plop! A small Christmas tree light bulb sailed across the room and landed at Regina's feet.

"Where did that come from?" she asked. "Hey, will it light up if I pick it up. It was ice cold. "Whoever did that, it was funny."

"That's a parlor trick. We want something more serious. Little stuff like that doesn't impress me," Eric taunted.

"What's the heaviest thing they've thrown, Anita?" Regina asked.

I was ready to say the wooden scrub brush when Chris piped up.

"Me," he said.

We all laughed. We then gathered our chairs to form a circle.

"Let's leave Chris alone," Regina, laughed again. "Throw something we can use, like a hundred dollar bill."

I laughed with her. "I'll take some of that."

"Come on. Man up. Is that all you have? Walk across the room!" Eric said impatiently.

"Elaine, are you getting the same two people? Are they the ones throwing things in the basement?" Regina asked.

"They are both standing aloof from me," Elaine replied.

There were several minutes of silence.

"I want to see something good. Throw a chair, move the curtains or levitate something," Regina demanded.

"I am coming back with a camera to place in every nook and cranny. You better cooperate with me or face my wrath," Eric said loudly.

I didn't know what to make of all this. Were they kidding? First, they seemed to be enjoying themselves almost mocking the spirits and now they were demanding that the spirits do parlor tricks and were upset when they didn't perform on cue. It didn't seem very professional to me. I was getting angry over how the investigation was taking an uneasy turn. They were asking for ghostly activity by threatening them. This could be dangerous and I was worried about our safety.

They thought they heard a rustling sound in the corner, but found nothing. They continued to investigate a little while longer and at 11:30 P.M., they decided to pack up and leave. I had become very uncomfortable, so was relieved at their departure.

"We'll be back to investigate further, Anita, we promise. We got such a late start we are going to call it a night," Regina said.

"We need to go through all the evidence we hoped we captured and organize our team members for the next time we come over," Eric said. "We'll be in touch."

I handed them an envelope with a donation for their organization. They had a policy of not accepting money for the actual investigating, but they gladly accepted donations towards their traveling expenses, if someone wished to do so. They thanked me and we followed them out the door. It had finally stopped raining, but the air was very humid.

Regina and Elaine hugged me as they got into their van, while Chris shook hands with Eric. When Regina asked me if she could have the can of soda, she had left on the side table, I ran in to get it. There was a pair of vintage woman's sunglasses near the soda and I figured they were either Regina's or Elaine's.

I handed Regina the can of soda and the glasses. "I think these glasses are yours," I said.

"They aren't mine, Anita. Are they yours, Elaine?" Regina asked.

"No, I've never seen them before," she answered.

"That's strange, I've never seen them before either," I said. They looked vintage and from the 1960's by their style. "They were right next to your soda."

Regina and Elaine just looked at each other - then the three drove off into the night.

—◊—

A week went by before we heard from E.R.I.E. In the meantime, Chris and I reviewed our tape and were astonished by the EVPs and the other noises we captured. We were also privy to the conversation that Eric and Elaine thought they were having privately. We heard them complain that our haunting didn't have enough activity for them and worse. We learned that they wondered if we were lying, or if Chris had thrown the key at Eric and that infuriated us. Where was their objectivity? Why weren't they being upfront with us about their feelings?

"I think they were just shining us along, Mom."

I agreed with him. "What kind of scientific approach is that? Just because something didn't knock Eric down or levitate for his wife, doesn't mean there's nothing worth investigating. How could you hit Eric in the back of the neck when I was sitting right by you? I would have seen you do that. They weren't even there that long. What a waste of our time!"

A few days later, Eric left a message on my answering machine saying that they hoped to come back to Paul's house and for us to get in touch with them. Given their attitudes and conversation recorded, I was surprised and a bit mystified but I returned the call. I spoke with Regina and her response was more what I'd expected - they didn't want to come back for another investigation. When I asked her what evidence they had picked up, she gave me the excuse that "their computers were down." How convenient. What was their game?

"We'll let you know what we found, but it's going to take a few weeks. Just finish cleaning up the house, Anita. Strip it bare and I think you'll be ok."

"So, you're not coming back?" I wanted her confirmation.

"No, I don't think it's necessary. They'll go away because there won't be anything for them to be attached to." She closed by reiterating that we should look for someone to bless the house before we sold it.

"Oh...ok, thanks for the advice and for coming to the house," I said.

I didn't want them back so I didn't press the issue.

We never heard from E.R.I.E again.

—ɯ—

This was our first dealing with investigators working in the field of the paranormal and it left a nasty taste in our mouths. We had called them to help us because they said they were professionals and we were sorely disappointed in how they treated our situation. We still wanted answers about what was happening in the house.

Just like someone who has an illness that doctors can't agree on, I wanted a second opinion. I was going to do more research to find local ghost investigators in our area and find the right group for us. I wasn't going to give up, but time was running out. We had gotten word from Stan, the real estate agent, that the first potential buyers for the house weren't able to get the right financing, so the deal was off. However, a local contractor had contacted him, through Paul's lawyer, and he was very interested in the house "as is." We could possibly be making a settlement as early as the end of October.

If this happened, Chris and I had only weeks to finish at the house before the new owners took possession. I couldn't, in all good conscience, sell a haunted house to an unsuspecting buyer. I had to try to do what I could to get the house "cleared" of its spirited inhabitants. I was worried and prayed for guidance.

"God, Paul, tell me. How I can help you?"

Chapter 27

ALL IN THE FAMILY

August 26th

Chris and I went to Paul's house again to clean out the last remnants of items in the dining room credenza and breakfront. I packed up the rest of the dishes and Chris piled up the hundreds of post cards he had discovered in a drawer on the dining room table. As Chris separated the cards for sorting, a travel brochure for Mexico turned up on the table. Chris asked me where it came from and I told him I had no idea. Could our ghosts be starting up again?

He found a cassette tape while he sorted the card and read it aloud to me. It was from *The Sound of Music*. Chris read the titles to the music on the tape and asked me about the song title: *How do you solve a problem like Maria?*

"It's from the show, Chris. The song goes like this…" I sang the first few lines from the song for him for fun. I reminded him that when he was little, I had taken him to see Rose's mother sing and perform as the Mother Abbess at a local stage production of the musical. She had a beautiful singing voice.

When I walked into the living room to get a box, a photo slide floated past me and landed on the floor. I held up the slide to the picture window to see what it was.

I couldn't believe my eyes. "Chris, take a look at this slide. What do you see?"

He took it from me and looked at it in the light. "Looks like it is some scene inside of a church, but taken from above. Someone is walking down the aisle."

"Yes, I recognize the scene. It's Julie Andrews as the bride, Maria, walking down the aisle to her waiting husband, Captain von Trapp in an Austrian Cathedral."

"So?"

"Don't you see? It's a slide from the movie, *The Sound of Music*. As Maria walks down the aisle, the nuns sing the song, *How Do You Solve a Problem like Maria*. I just sang some of the song."

"That's crazy."

"It's not crazy, it's incredible. Paul heard everything we just said."

August 28th

Mrs. Jaeger made her presence known to us today. Chris and I were picking up some junk to put into trash bags, including some cracked pink plastic coasters. Activity started in the kitchen while I washed my hands for lunch. A slide hit me at the sink and when I looked at it, I saw that it was of Mrs. Jaeger.

"Maybe she didn't like you throwing out those old dish towels and expired medicine bottles from under the sink, Mom."

"Too bad, this stuff is disgusting."

"Hey, what just hit me?" Chris asked as he picked up one of the pink plastic coasters. "This was in the trash. Are you ghosts serious? This thing is cracked. What good is it?"

"You're trying to rationalize with dead people, Chris. Good luck."

Suddenly I felt a presence and something like an electric charge, and saw a black shadow figure standing right next to me. I jumped back instinctively and screamed as the trash bag rustled and something darted out from it and landed in the dining room. Chris ran to retrieve the object. It was another pink plastic coaster.

I was still trying to recover from the shock of the shadowy presence when I shouted, "Ok, keep your crappy coasters!" I dropped them on the kitchen counter.

Later that afternoon, Chris and I found Mrs. Jaeger's wedding gown when we cleared out one of the last wall cabinets in the basement. It was folded into a small box and when I first saw it, I thought it was just some old fabric. I quickly took it upstairs and laid it out on the couch. As I unfolded it, I found that the veil and headdress were still intact under the gown. The green silk floral wreath reminded me of something. *It's just like Julie Andrews's bridal head piece in The Sound of Music,* I thought.

I spread the white lace and silk gown out carefully along with the veil headpiece and looked at it for a moment. I admired the workmanship on the gown and saw a small sprig of silk flowers pinned to the bodice of the dress. Was this a German custom? Perhaps it was a good luck charm. I hoped that Carl would want to keep it for his daughter. She was Mrs. Jaeger's only granddaughter.

Flop!

I turned around and saw a plastic laminated card in the middle of the living room floor. I picked it up and as I turned it over the hairs in the back of my neck stood up. I saw that it was the prayer card from Mrs. Jaeger's funeral.

August 31st

Chris and I were in the garden house to finish cleaning up. We found books and magazines in the back cabinets that still needed to be given away. The counter top had miscellaneous junk on it and I proceeded to clean it off, dumping the items into a trash bag. We hadn't been in the shed for more than ten minutes when we heard something splash.

"Hey, what the...?" Chris exclaimed, looking down at his shoe.

We looked on the floor and found two small puddles of blue-green liquid near him.

"I think it's ink, but I'm not sure," I said. "Is there a pen around that's leaking?"

Chris and I looked around the small area. "No, there's a paint brush on the floor. He picked it up. "The brush is dripping with that blue-green stuff. Son of a gun! That's how it splashed. It even made a pattern on the floor."

I looked at it closely and realized what had happened. *Something* had dipped the brush in an invisible liquid and splashed it - at Chris.

We continued to empty out the back cabinets and packed the last of the magazines in the boxes.

"What the hell, man?" Chris yelled. He jumped back and stepped towards me. "It's that blue stuff again. Crap, look it's all over my socks."

I looked where Chris was pointing to bluish streaks splashed all over his white athletic socks.

"Where's it coming from?" I asked him. "Look around to see if there's an open container or something."

Chris walked around and found more of the same liquid pooled in the corner of the room. He picked up what looked like a ripped balloon dripping with the blue-green liquid.

"The ghosts have officially gone porno, Mom," he said.

"What are you talking about?" I looked more closely. "Oh, my God, is that what I think it is?"

"Yeah, it's a freaking condom. This is so disgusting. What's a ghost doing with something like this?"

"I don't know. Which ghost are we talking about?"

"It was aimed at me," Chris said. "Maybe it was the father. This was his domain."

This was too weird.

"Who's going to believe this?" I asked Chris.

"No one, but the tape recorder is on so hopefully we captured something."

I walked out of the garden house to get a wet paper towel to clean up the mess. As I walked pass the trash bags something caught my eye. An old plastic bottle of plant food I remembered throwing out in the trash now lay on the lawn. I picked it up and saw it was half-empty. I remembered the bottle being full. I'd thought of keeping it for my plants at home, but the lid was rusted shut because it hadn't ever been opened, so I just tossed it.

Oh, my God. That was it! The same blue-green color liquid had stained Chris' socks.

"What in the world?" Chris asked when I showed him the bottle. "Can this get any weirder?"

"More like X-rated weird."

We wound up in the Jaeger's kitchen and Chris tried to wipe the stains from his socks. "This isn't going to come off, it's permanent."

I was getting our things together to get ready to leave when a yellow sponge flew into the air and a pencil hit the dining room door as I walked through.

"Let's get out of here," I said, grabbing my handbag.

Chris was getting up from the kitchen table when a small bucket of slides that were on the table, flew right at his face

"Son of a bitch!" he yelled angrily. "Don't worry, I'm going! No one wants to be in your crappy house."

Just then, a key whizzed by Chris' arm and hit the wall.

"Go, Chris. Don't pick up the slides. Get out of here before you get hurt."

He ran out the door and I quickly set the alarm and left.

Chapter 28

CHILLING EVPS

September 3ʳᵈ

September arrived and we knew that our time in the house would end in a matter of weeks, so capturing and recording EVPs was high on our priority list.

We put the new digital recorder we'd purchased in different locations around the house as we worked. Several incidents stood out that day and later on, upon reviewing the digital recorder, the noises and voices captured reinforced what we had experienced at a specific time and our reactions. The recording lasted 53 minutes and 36 seconds. In that period, we captured an average one EVP per minute. Within the first seconds after we set foot in the kitchen a pen came flying through the air.

: 21 "You want…"

: 31 "Get out!"

: 58 Bang!

Chris heard a bang in the mother's bedroom and went to investigate. While there, a spool of red thread was thrown on the floor.

"Mrs. Jaeger, are you in the room with us?"

2:36 "Yeah."

Chris and I were packing some breakables in a box.

3:56 Bang!

3:59 "Hans...Bang!....Jaeger!" Sounded like a cane hitting the floor to emphasize something said.

4:08 High pitch sound.

4:23 "Get out!"

4:40 "Get out or I'll f**k you!"

4:52 "...get out!"

Chris got hit in the hand with a pen.

5:26 "Get the hell out!"

Chris and I were startled when a wall plug hit a lamp, but did not break it.

7:23 "I hit it."

7:37 "Now you're done."

7:53 "Help."

8:08 "Tell them that."

8:25 Strange sounding noise.

8:28 "Wait till the devil comes, he'll stop you."

9:09 "Please... get out."

A yellow top to a magic marker was thrown. I got angry and yelled at them to stop the activity.

11:30 "She's mad!"

A photo slide landed on the carpet, and I picked it up and held the slide up to the light. It was a slide of Paul taken in front of some Indian ruins.

"Is that you, Paul?" I asked.

12:20 "Yes."

"Are these getting packed up for that store, Grandmom's Attic?" Chris asked.

12:42 "Grandmom's Attic." (They were imitating him.)

Chris once again was a target for another object thrown.

"Yeah, throw stuff, you ghost bastards. Give me your shoes!" Chris taunted.

"Ouch!"

13:53 Bump

14:04 "I got him."

"Are you all right?" I asked him.

"I'm ok."

"What hit you anyway, Chris?"

He picked up the brown object. "It's a shoe horn."

"That's too funny," I laughed.

15:14 "I want you now."

15:24 "AHHH...I want them out."

15:28 Sounds of a song bird chirping. We did find parakeet cages in the basement. Mrs. Jaeger loved birds and had some as pets.

15:45 "Hit."

16:07 "Ha, ha, ha, ha."

"Mom, do you want me to take out those boxes?"

16:22 "Take it home."

16:52 BANG!

"Yes, they go in the garage."

While we were taking the boxes out through the kitchen door, a red pencil hit my leg. Chris left the recorder on the counter top in the kitchen when we went outside.

18:09 Sound of an intake of breath then the sounds of heavy breathing.

19:15 "The god is coming."

19:45 Sounds of multiple people talking.

19:48 "Help."

19:58 laughing.

The kitchen became very active with slides in a bucket, a red lid to a can and small light bulbs being throw around the room.

20:03 deep voice "...Atten...hut."

20:04 sounds of people marching.

20:25 weird noises

20:35 Sounds as if there were airplanes droning overhead.

22:05 "Get them!"

22:49 Sounds of people talking

As we entered the room, a key was thrown in the middle of the room.

23:18 "Get out!"

23:23 Sounds of someone laughing

23:51 "Sigh"

24:11 Bang

Someone or something removed the dimmer switch knob and turned off the lights again.

24:20 laughter

25:23 "Get the hell out!"

Chris and I were standing in the living room. He held the digital recorder in one hand while walking around the room. We heard an unearthly noise coming from the direction of the kitchen.

"What the hell was that?" I asked.

"Can you talk into my recorder?" Chris asked. "Make your presence known."

25:28 Click, click

We heard a very loud strange vibrating noise that sounded like it was coming from the walls all around the room. It only lasted a few seconds.

26:28 AHHHHHHHHHH

"What's the sound?" I asked. "That was really weird."

"Can you make that sound again?" Chris asked. "Can you do that again?"

27:09 ahhhhhhhh....AHHHHHHHHHHHHHHH

"OH MY GOD!" Chris yelled. "That sounded like a freight train coming through here. The whole room vibrated! That was kind of creepy."

"Do you hear that humming sound?" I asked Chris. "Sounds like a motor running."

We both followed the sound into the kitchen and found that the freezer door was wide open.

29:46 Bang!

A can of baby powder flew out of the bathroom and hit the wall.

32:26 the door to the hall linen close opened and slammed shut.

38:28 we saw a flickering gold light dancing on the wall opposite the hall closet.

38:40 Sounds of music

39:47 cuckoo clock sounds

41:19 "Get out."

41:39 "Get the hell out!"

42:07 Sounds of heavy breathing

43:17 "Get out of the house."

A small thimble was thrown at me.

44:15 a non-human sounding laughter

46:40 "Sigh"

Chris was in Paul's room with his recorder. Suddenly he came running out in a panic.

"The painting moved. I'm out of here!"

Chris ran by me fast and to the kitchen. As he ran by the kitchen table, a small green bucket with over fifty pens, pencils and other stationary items flew at him and crashed to the floor.

"Aggghhhhh!" Chris yelled.

"What happened?"

Chris was out of breath as I met him outside. "I asked Paul to give me a sign and the painting that was leaning against the wall fell against his bed, and now this! They don't want us here. I'm not coming back in, let's go!"

"But I thought you wanted to help me bury Heidi the cat. Her ashes are still on the shelf." I called out after him.

49:15 "Sigh"

49:37 something said unintelligible, bang

50:43 "Get out!"

52:12 "I'm coming over tonight."

52:42 "Now."

52:43 "Take the cat, Heidi."

September 15th

Our tape was supposed to last for two hours, but after ten minutes we experienced interference and the rest of the tape was ruined. This is all we captured, in the living room, in that short amount of time.

:20 *"Yeah"*

:34 *"Change the crib."*

:45 *"Get the hell out of here"* (*followed by a long vibrating noise*)

1:20 *"I'm dead, he just told them"*

1:32 *"Get out"*

4:26 Weird sound

4:35 *"Get the hell out of the house"* (*banging to emphasize what was being said*)

4:55 *"Get the house sold"*

5:01 People talking loud

5:03 *"You...are ordered out...get out!"*

5:05 *"Krakow...death toll"*

5:553 *Thump...thump...*(*banging on drums?*)

6:04 sounds of people/soldiers marching

6:08 *"I know them"*

6:18 door closes in hallway

6:35 *"Come Kevin...do you know them?"*

6:40 *"I'm Kevin and Michael"*

I'm talking to my son as I am packing certain items up.

7:18 *"No. no"*

"I'm giving these to the Purple Heart," I said to Chris and Danny.

7:40 *"No"*

8:44 *"Stop the truck"*

9:02 *"Get them out of here!"*

9:13 *Bells sounding and then bangs*

"What are you doing with these, Mom?"

"I have to put those away."

9:46 *"No"*

9:50 *"Okay"*

10:03 Sounds of static and high pitch unintelligible strange noises interfered with the rest of the tape.

September 23rd

We weren't going to let the supernatural interfere with our recording. We pushed on and had Danny with us as a witness for our recording session which lasted about 23 minutes. We started working in another storage shed that had to be cleaned out. When we found it a month earlier, we thought it belonged to the neighbor in the back, but surprise! It belonged to Paul. We were glad to have Danny's help. Little did we know that after what happened that afternoon he would never come back to Paul's house.

We went into the kitchen for cold drinks and snacks and then set up the digital recorder on the dining room table. Two minutes into the recording, the poltergeist activity began to happen.

2:00 "Want a cookie?"

2:02 "How about this!"

"Whoa! I just got hit in the face with some paper clips." Danny yelled and ran out of the kitchen.

"Oh, for God's sake, they're starting again," I said. "You ok, Danny?"

2:06 "Help"

2:29 "No"

"Yeah, I just never expected that."

"This is a psycho haunted house, Danny. You know you always have to expect the unexpected," I said.

"You're right, Miss A."

We still had books by the dozens to repack after Carl had picked through them and decided he had enough and didn't want the rest.

"I'll make room here, if you start packing up those nature books, Danny," Chris said. "Here," he held out some boxes. "Take these."

4:05 "Stop them...have some fun"

Several books flew across the living room.

"You know where you can shove these books, don't you?" Chris shouted to the ghosts.

5:03 "Up your...ass
5:12 Cackling-type laughter
5:26 "Helll...p" (long drawn out)
5:44 "Get out"
5:52 "He wants to blow you"
"What's this book, Mom? Whale songs?"
6:09 "Yeah"
"It's a kid's book."
6:35 "Help them."
"Here you go Danny, some Crown Royal for you," Chris handed him a tiny bottle of Canadian whiskey. "Drink up my man!"
7:33 "Yeah, drink up"
Danny walked over to get the bottle and a pillow from the chair in back of him flew over his head.
"Hey, what's going on?" Danny asked and started to laugh.
"Whatayoudoin, Danny?" Chris laughed.
8:58 "I'm the one who threw it"
9:55 knocks on the floor
10:38 Music is heard.
11:37 More slides and paper clips were thrown on the floor.
We continued to pack things and take them out of the house. When we got back to the living room there was a trail of slides leading right to the parents' bedroom.
"Someone has too much time on their hands," Chris said.
13:00 "Sigh"
13:24 "Get out now."
13:42 "I feel bad"
13:52 Sounds of something dragging.
14:09 "Yes"
14:26 "Help"
14:45 Pen got thrown, red of course.
15:16 "It's not over"
16:53 "Sigh"
17:06 "Help...me" (child's voice)

17:06 A cry, sounded like an animal.

17:53 "Move?"

"Here, Chris, take the projector screen out to the garage," I said to him.

17:58 "No!" (a deep robotic sounding voice)

18:32-19:02 Music...then ringing sound...ding dong...(doorbell?) "That's mine"... Ding...dong...music (was this evidence of over 30 seconds of residual haunting?)

"We need to get those other boxes in the basement, guys," I said

19:35 knocking sounds

Chris and Danny followed me through the kitchen to the basement door. I went first to put the lights on with Chris behind me. Danny hesitated at the top of the steps and asked me where the knocks were coming from.

"Who cares? Let them knock," I said sarcastically.

20:05 SLAM

Suddenly, the basement door slammed right in Danny's face, separating us and leaving him stranded in the kitchen. Danny was startled and frantically tried to open the door.

"Oh, Jesus!" Chris exclaimed and grabbed for the doorknob on our side. He jiggled the knob but it was frozen.

"Agghhhh, it won't open, I can't get the door open!" Danny kept yelling.

"Oh my God!" I screamed. "Danny, are you ok?"

The doorknob wouldn't budge and as we pounded on the door we heard Danny yell that something was in the kitchen with him. We heard a horrible, high pitched, non-human voice screech, *"Oh...my...God!"*

It was imitating me.

We finally got the door opened just in time to see Danny bolt out the kitchen door.

"Hey, man...you all right?" Chris called out to him.

"Sorry, but that's it. I'm not going back in there," Danny yelled as he made his way to his car. He kept shaking his head.

21:07 "Look down"

"I have to go," Danny said.

21:11 "We won't let you"

"What did you see?" I asked him frantically

21:20 "...behind you" (whisper)

"I was trying to open the door, but the knob was frozen. I felt something breathing on my neck and when I turned around...whatever it was...it wasn't human!"

Chapter 29

SPIRIT TURBULENCE

October 1st

"I can't believe that it's almost over, Mom!" Chris said, as we drove from the lawyer's office to Paul's house.

We had just signed a tentative agreement with the new contractors, the first step in the sale of the house. It had been one of the easier transactions in the last nine months in dealing with Paul's estate. I liked the prospective buyers, Tom and his business partner John, immediately, and they made a decent offer without any complicated stipulations. They had left a down payment with the contract that morning at the lawyer's office and we eagerly signed the agreement.

If all went according to plan, the contract would be finalized by October 30 and the house would be theirs.

"I always said there was no way I wanted us to still be working in that house on Halloween," I said. "This is going to work out perfectly."

We were going to check on the house and meet with a local antiques dealer who was interested in buying some of the heavy metal cabinets in the basement. I was glad to get whatever I could for them and for the parents' bedroom furniture. They were some of the last big items removed from Paul's house. The rest of the water damaged built-in bookcases, shelves and appliances were going to be scrapped, since the contractors were planning to gut the basement, the kitchen and the bathroom. I had a charity in mind that might be willing to pick up some other miscellaneous items, including the dining room and living room furniture, if the antiques dealer did not want them.

We entered the house at around 11:30 AM, and as soon as we walked in the kitchen, we heard the sound of water splashing below us.

"What the hell is going on?" Chris asked

We became alarmed so we checked under the kitchen sink first and then dashed to the basement. Water was pouring through the first floor ceiling, down the paneled walls of the basement steps and onto the concrete basement floor. Half the basement was flooded with an inch of water!

"Oh my God!" I screamed. "Where's it coming from?"

We ran back upstairs. Had someone left the water running in the upstairs bathroom sink? I knew no one had used the bathroom when we were there only two days earlier and I had checked all the rooms before we left. When we reached the hallway, I caught a sickening sight. Water was gushing onto the bathroom floor, flooding the room and splashing into the hallway, soaking the carpet and hardwood floor underneath. I looked, saw the sink, and noticed that the faucets weren't turned on.

It looked like the water was coming from the toilet so Chris quickly reached down and shut off the water valve under the toilet tank. He lifted the lid and saw that the tank was empty.

"The water's been constantly filling up in the tank as it was emptying. So there has to be a leak, but I don't see it." Chris said.

I picked up the sopping wet throw rug to put it in the tub.

A hard banging sound vibrated under my feet.

Bang! Bang! Bang!

"Jesus, something is trying to come up through the floor!" I screamed.

Didn't something like this happen in the movie, Poltergeist? I thought.

We didn't wait to see. Chris ran back to the basement to see if the water had stopped flowing, while I went to the phone in the dining room to call my mother who had the emergency number of a plumber my family used. While I was on the phone, Chris yelled up to me.

"There's someone walking through the water, Mom!" He sounded terrified!

Boom ... Boom ... BOOM!

Unseen fists were pounding the paneled walls leading down to the basement. It thundered in my ears.

"Call the police, Anita," my mother said on the other end of the phone. She was worried. She could hear the terrible noise over the phone "Call 911!"

"What am I going to tell them, Mom? They'll think I'm crazy."

My hands were shaking as I managed to find a piece of paper to write the plumber's number. A small note pad hit me on the head when I hung up the phone.

"Hey, cut it out," I yelled. I'd have laughed if I wasn't so frightened.

I picked up the receiver again to call the plumber, but there was no dial tone. I tried several more times until I realized the phone was dead! We were being cut off from any help! What were we going to do? I ran downstairs to use Chris' cell phone. He was frantically trying to swish the water away with a broom to form a channel to the drain.

"What did you see in the water?" I asked him. I could see the fear in his face.

"Someone was walking through it. I could see bubbles as this dark *thing* went through the water, making a pounding noise. Did you call the plumber?"

"The phone's dead upstairs. I'll call from your cell."

I tried to call the plumber's emergency number, but it would not connect. I tried again and got his answering machine, leaving a message for him to call me back ASAP.

"That's some great emergency number," Chris said with disgust. He continued to mop the remaining cascading water. Swear poured down his red face.

The water had slowed, but was still dripping from the ceiling so I put some buckets down to catch the water. I grabbed a broom and started to sweep some of the water from the bottom of the steps over towards the sump pump drain. We had no other way of removing the water since the laundry tubs and their drains were gone. I was grateful that the antique dealer wasn't expected for a least another hour, so I hoped to have the majority of the puddles reduced to damp stains.

Chris and I were sweating and coughing in the damp, moldy basement. We were starting to make progress when all hell broke loose - a seven-foot piece of aluminum duct pipe came out of nowhere and landed in front of us.

"Jesus H. Christ!" Chris yelled. "That just missed us."

Suddenly the three buckets I had place under the drips, levitated and were thrown across the room, spilling all the collected water. "Stop it! Dear God, please protect us. Help us!" I called out.

A broom crashed near us.

"They're mad, Mom. They didn't want us to sell the house."

I looked at Chris, who was standing near the wooden partition he had almost taken down when he was attacked in August. I blinked twice and couldn't believe my eyes. The wooden studs holding up the partition and part of the ceiling were stating to move out of alignment, as if someone were kicking them.

"Chris, move!" I screamed. "The whole damn ceiling is going to come down."

A horrendous banging sound thundered all around us. First, a piece of tile ripped off the ceiling from the other side of the basement and then a large wooden beam smacked against the wall.

"They're trying to destroy the whole place, Mom!"

"Let them, as long as they don't take us with them. Let's get out of here!"

We flew upstairs and outside to the car. It had been twenty minutes since I'd called the emergency number and the plumber never called back. We were hot, sweaty, wet and terrified.

"I'm calling the lawyer. He has to know what's happening here."

Jeff wasn't in, but his assistant, Linda, was very concerned when I told her what was happening at Paul's house. She could hear the terror in my voice.

"Look, Anita, I'll call our law office's emergency plumber and have him there in ten minutes. I'm on my way over, ok?" Linda said.

Linda arrived before the plumber, Scott, got there. She had never been to Paul's house, but had heard some of our stories about the paranormal events we had been experiencing there for the last five months during our meetings with Jeff. She knew by the honest conviction we exhibited when we told our stories that they had to be true. I could always count on her for a sympathetic ear. She and Jeff believed us.

"What's happening here, guys?" She asked.

"What's *not* happening here?" Chris answered.

Linda saw from our faces that we were showing signs of battle fatigue. She cast a wary eye around the room as she entered the kitchen with us.

"What's that smell?" she asked.

"It actually doesn't smell that bad now. You should have been here at the beginning," Chris said.

"I can't imagine," Linda said.

We showed her to the damaged bathroom and realized there was a trail of red rubber bands leading us there.

"What the...?" Linda looked stunned. We finished explaining about the violent activity we had experienced during the last hour and a half. When we turned back toward the living room, a black wallet flew by Linda and landed on the sofa. By the look on her face, we knew she had seen it too. Then, we heard what sounded like a loud moan.

"Oh, God, I need a cigarette," she said as she made her way quickly out the kitchen door.

Scott arrived soon after that and we showed him to the bathroom. He was perplexed when he examined the toilet looking for the leak.

"Here it is," he said and pointed to the damage. "The toilet tank is cracked right down the middle. The water has been flowing from the crack."

"How did that happen?' I asked him. Even with him pointing at it, I could hardly see the crack.

"Strange, because you have to exert a lot of force and pressure to crack a porcelain tank like that. Does anyone have access to the house when you're not here?" Scott asked.

"No, no one else has been here since Monday. We were here working outside and never even used the bathroom that day. I did come in the house briefly to check things and I would have heard it if the water was running. Everything was fine," I said as I turned to Linda who had found the courage to re-enter the house.

"That's really strange. Now, I know it's an older toilet and they're known to crack with sudden temperature changes, but it's eighty-five degrees outside and around seventy degrees inside, so that's not it," Scott said.

"Well, strange doesn't begin to describe this house," Chris mumbled to Linda.

She looked with a half-bemused smile.

"I mean you'd have to throw your full body weight against the tank to crack it that way. I actually had a client who did just that. They stumbled in the dark in the middle of the night and cracked their toilet. I don't know what else could have done it."

We knew, though.

"Let me check out the heater and electrical outlets down in the basement," Scott said and we held our collective breath as he headed that way.

He reported to us that the water had not damaged them and that the wooden ceiling would dry out and probably not be replaced.

"This wasn't leaking for very long until you discovered it. I'd say maybe less than two days. It could have been worse," Scott said after he examined the rafters.

"Linda, when you talk to Jeff please tell him I feel bad about all this damage since we just signed the paper work for the contractors. We had no idea that this had happened until we got here today," I said

"I will, Anita, but don't worry. From what I understand, the contractors will be redoing much of the house. Tom and John are good guys," Linda said. "I don't think it will be a problem."

"Well, I don't think there's anything else for me to do," Scott said. "If you want me to replace the toilet I could, but it would be a waste of time seeing the contractors are only going to tear it out again to replace it with their new bathroom fixtures."

Scott said we could still use the damaged toilet; all we had to do was put a bucket of water in the tank and flush it when needed. I didn't think Chris and I would use the "haunted toilet" anytime soon.

After the plumber left, Paul's phone rang. I was startled when I heard it because it meant it was working again. It was Walter, the antiques dealer, calling to tell me he was on his way.

Linda stayed in the living room with Chris while I showed Walter the cabinets in the basement. The floor was just damp now, the water reduced to several small puddles. I put a fan on to help dry up the floor. As we walked around a corner of the basement, I heard something be thrown down the steps. Walter didn't interrupt his conversation, so I figured he didn't hear the smack on the concrete floor. I quickly discovered a small red leather manicure kit and ignored it. *If he thinks this place is haunted he may not want to buy any of the furniture,* I thought.

I didn't miss a beat and we continued our discussion about what he'd buy and how much he'd give me for the pieces. We went outside to the garage and he wrote down the other items he was interested in. After about twenty minutes, he left with the promise that he'd be back the next week with a truck for the furniture.

I went inside and heard Linda and Chris talking. As I walked in to the living room, she was on her way out again for another cigarette.

I looked at Chris and asked him what had happened since I'd been occupied with the antiques dealer.

"Let's just say Linda has been fully initiated into our haunted house," Chris said, half-laughing.

"What?" I asked.

"You know the usual. Red pens, slides, paper clips thrown around the room. She really freaked out when she heard the cat scratching and meowing. Then, when I was showing her the bedrooms, the door to the cat room slammed shut and she'd really had it. I don't think she's coming back in."

We walked across the street to Linda's car just as she was taking the last drag on her cigarette and putting the butt out with her heel.

"I can't believe it. I was standing right next to Chris and all these things started flying around the room. In addition, the noises are unbelievable! I don't know how you've been able to work all these months here with all this crazy stuff going on," she said.

I leaned against the car. "Faith? Curiosity? Stupidity? I don't know, Linda. Now, I'm just worried about selling the place before we can get someone here to "clear" it of the spirits," I said.

"Mom contacted another paranormal investigative team," Chris told Linda. "She's waiting to hear back from them this weekend."

"Chris' boss, Kent, heard about this woman who is really good and is the founder of Tri-County Paranormal Investigators. I hope they can help because I'm afraid time is running out." I gazed over at Paul's house.

"What if you can't get the spirits out in time, Anita? It's not your fault. Jeff knows what a super-human feat you've accomplished here in such a short time. He said that in all his years of dealing with estates he has never seen such a complicated one. Moreover, you did ninety-nine percent of the work! How much more can you do?" Linda asked.

I had tears in my eyes. "Linda, Paul needs my help. There is something he's trying desperately to tell me and I just need the right psychic medium to communicate with him. I have to try this one last time."

"Well, I'll tell you I don't think I could have done this. Paul was lucky to have you because you're one hell of a friend," Linda said and hugged me.

"Thanks, Linda," I said.

"Hey? What about me?" Chris asked in a mocked tone of hurt.

"You too, Chris," Linda hugged him and then got into her car. "Just promise me you both will be careful. Jeff wouldn't want to probate *your* wills any time soon!"

She waved goodbye as we crossed the street back to Paul's house. Chris' cell phone rang. It was Pete, our plumber. He was sorry he hadn't gotten our message sooner and didn't know why the emergency message had gone to his voice mail instead of directly to his cell phone. Did we need him to come out?

"No, Pete, it's taken care of, thanks," Chris replied. He hung up the phone and looked at me. "Funny, Mom, he said that never happened before."

We walked into the kitchen. "It seems that "never happened before" happens all the time here."

Everything was very still and quiet. When we turned out the lights in the basement and started up the stairs, I noticed something hanging from the pull string on one of the lights. It was a white fabric dove. I looked closer and saw it was attached to the string with a blue plastic clothespin. It swayed back and forth from an invisible hand.

"Mom, maybe it's a peace offering."

"Dear God, I hope so."

Chapter 30

SAGE ADVICE

"Hello? This is Laurie Hull. I'm returning your call about a problem you are having related to a haunting?"

I was so glad to get her call several days after the last violent confrontation we'd had at Paul's house. I felt an instant connection with her warm mannerism and friendly personality.

"I understand you've had some extreme paranormal experiences?"

"Where do I begin, Laurie?"

We talked for the next half hour and I expressed my reservations about working with another investigative team considering my experience with the last group.

"I'm very sorry to hear about what you've been put through. Some people in our field are thrill seekers who are looking for quick fame associated with a unique haunting, sometimes at the expense of the client. They want to make a lot of money. Just because people have an interest in the supernatural, buy some expensive equipment and print up business cards doesn't make them professional investigators."

"How long have you been involved with the world of the paranormal Laurie?"

"Actually, I've been a psychic medium all my life and founded the group in 1982 before it became popular to be a ghost hunter. My associates are gifted, professional and trustworthy. We volunteer our time to help people like you. Unfortunately, ghost groups are very popular right now and popping up everywhere so you have to be careful about whom you are dealing with."

"I wish I knew about you first, Laurie. I could have saved myself some problems with the first group I had at the house."

"Well, I'm familiar with that group you mentioned. Umm...are you near your computer and have it on?"

"Yes."

"I want you to look up E.R.I.E.'s web site. I think you'll find something on there that will interest you."

I typed in the web site address.

"Click on the link that says, Recent Investigations," Laurie said.

I clicked on and was soon looking at pictures of Paul's kitchen, living room and basement. Though they kept our location secret, they stated that they had done a full investigation at the house that night and described the paranormal evidence and events they had collected and experienced. There were even pictures of the objects that had been thrown that night, on the site. They finally said they were planning a return visit to help cleanse the house of its spirits. What a joke! They had never asked for our permission to use any of this, despite their telling us they would not, as part of their mission statement to protect a client's privacy.

"Boy, they made us feel as if we had wasted their time."

"I've run into this group before. I've heard some complaints about them."

"I don't know who to trust now, Laurie. I had a few calls in to the clergy, but I've been ignored. No one wants to get involved. Should I try again to get a priest to bless the house?"

"I wouldn't. Having a priest bless the house can actually make it worse. And don't believe the remedy of burning sage, or what is called smudging. It doesn't work. These actions can stir things up more on a very negative level. In fact, it can antagonize *them*."

"Really?"

"Believe me, Anita, I've seen it happen. If you want us to help you, we'd be glad to. We never charge for our services. We can try to connect with your friend and find out what he wants. I know you said it was urgent so I will get back to you in a day or so and see if I can set something up with some of my team for a visit to his house, Ok?"

"Yes, let's do it. Thanks so much, Laurie."

"One thing I have to tell you, Anita, is that there are no guarantees in dealing with spirits. They have their own agenda, and do things in their own time. Remember, they have eternity on their side, and we can't hurt or influence them, only suggest and guide them."

Laurie's last statement left me pondering the subject of immortality. I'd had several very good friends who died suddenly at a young age, but they never tried to contact me. Why was Paul haunting me? Would Laurie and her team be able to help solve this puzzle and end this nightmare finally?

Chapter 31

CROSSING OVER

I had been anxious all day. Chris and I were at Paul's house and Laurie and her team were scheduled to meet with us at 7:00 PM. Coincidentally, Laurie didn't live far from the house, which intrigued her. Familiar with the neighborhood, she would have never guessed that one of the modest ranch style houses was harboring such an unusual and intense mystery. My previous conversation with her left me feeling encouraged that I had finally found the right people to help us and that they would be sensitive to our unique situation.

This had to work.

They arrived right on time. Laurie introduced herself and the other members of her investigative team, Clare and her husband Randy. Laurie was younger than I had expected, very pretty with long dark hair and sparkling green eyes. Clare was an attractive woman also with long dark hair who wasn't exactly psychic like Laurie, but had certain abilities as a spirit adviser that would be needed in this case. Her husband Randy, also a psychic medium, was a gentle bear of a man with a graying beard and an easy laugh. Chris and I were at ease with them immediately, and felt that what we would reveal about our experiences in this house would be accepted in a non-judgmental, trustworthy manner.

We briefly showed them around the house and Randy started picking up his first impressions in the basement, where the activity had been so frequent.

"I have to say my feelings are that both you and your son have great energy and are very friendly people. That's a good thing because it will help with any negative energy that is here."

Clare picked up some high readings on her EMF detector and said that there were several spirits with us. She said that my friend wanted to communicate with us, but not through her or Laurie. He would feel more comfortable speaking through Randy. We then heard some tapping sounds above us.

"They went upstairs," she said.

We all went back upstairs to the living room. I was grateful that we still had some furniture left in the living room.

"Are they here?" I asked Clare. "I just felt a cold draft at my elbow."

"They came up here in an instant," she answered. "It's like *zip*, as quick as a thought they were up here ahead of us."

"I just heard someone behind me say *'help'*," Randy said.

"I heard that too, Randy," I said.

"That's interesting," Chris said.

We settled ourselves in the living room. Randy took a side chair near a table where I had set up an 8" x 10" framed picture of Paul in his best "Indiana Jones" hat, smiling in front of some South American Indian ruins. I sat on the other chair near the table while Laurie and Clare sat on the sofa.

Chris insisted on standing in the doorway to the hall opposite Randy, with his digital tape recorder. He laughingly said that he was standing guard, just in case. "We've had lots of stuff fly through this hall, in case you didn't know."

We didn't film this session because we were going to be in a dimly lit situation, as requested by Laurie, and Chris felt that his camera without the proper infrared film would be useless. The session began.

"Are you here with us, Paul?" Laurie asked. "Do you want to speak to us?"

For several minutes, there was complete silence. Then, I heard heavy breathing coming from Randy. His eyes were closed and he seemed to be going into a trance. Suddenly Randy coughed and Chris jumped; Randy awakened and laughed at his reaction. He then settled himself again and we waited nervously while Laurie began to ask her questions.

"Paul, please talk to us. We can help you if you're having problems being here."

Only Randy's very heavy, deep breathing broke the silence. Another minute went by and then Randy spoke, but I knew it was Paul.

"Why are you here?"

"We came here to help you," Laurie said.

"I'm very upset with myself."

"We don't want you to be upset. Who is speaking?" Laurie asked.

"My name is Paul."

"Hi Paul," Laurie said in a calm, soothing voice "We see your picture on the table. You look happy and you're standing near the Mayan Indian ruins I see in the back. I understand you liked studying the Mayans.

"Yes, I know."

"Anita and Chris have asked us to be here. We want to help. We are sorry your life was cut short. We want to know why you haven't moved into the light."

"Can't."

"Why can't you move on? Aren't your mother and father with you?"

"No."

"Are you the one throwing things to get Anita and Chris' attention?" Clare asked.

"I'm very upset."

"Is there a reason why you're upset and haven't moved on...into the light?" Laurie asked.

"Unfinished business."

"What is your unfinished business, Paul? Maybe we can help you with it," Clare emphasized.

"I didn't prepare for this."

"But Paul, how would you have prepared yourself?' Laurie sympathized.

"If..." cough...heavy breathing.

"Paul, can I send you some energy to help you talk?" Clare asked.

"Good...Ahhh...uhhh."

It sounded like Paul was straining through Randy's voice to get something out.

"There's an artifact...that you took home...that's not of this world."

"What!" I exclaimed. "What is he talking about?"

"Jesus," Chris said. "Is he serious?"

Laurie and Clare tried to calm us down, but I think they were just as stunned as we were by the sudden, unexpected revelation that came from nowhere.

"Can you tell us what it is, Paul?" Laurie asked.

"No."

"Paul, can you describe it to Anita?" Clare asked.

"Ummm...cough...it is like stone. It's similar to pottery, but...more like marble."

"Do you want Anita and Chris to find it?"

"The artifact is in the wrong hands. They shouldn't have it...not good for them."

"I have no idea what he's talking about," Chris said.

"Maybe I can draw it for you," Laurie suddenly volunteered. "I'm getting a picture of something. Do you guys have a piece of paper and pen?"

At that moment, a deep, unfamiliar voice was recorded on Chris' digital recorder. *"Don't draw it!"*

We waited as she drew the object. Randy still had his eyes closed and was still in a trance. Laurie made a depreciating laugh at her artistic skills.

"Don't laugh guys. I'm not an artist like Anita."

She showed the drawing to Chris and me but we didn't recognize the object at all.

"This is what I came up with. It's small with a slender body and a bulbous head with writing or designs on it. I don't know. Do you remember seeing anything like this in the house?"

"Nah," was the response we heard on Chris digital recorder.

"I found a lot of American Indian stuff stored in Paul's bedroom, but I don't remember seeing anything like that," I said.

"Mom, isn't there a rattle that maybe looks like that... it's got feathers?"

"No, it's not that. We have many Native American items stored away. Is there some kind of other world demon or evil spirit attached to one of the objects, Laurie?"

"That's what the other medium seemed to think," Chris added.

"I don't think there is. There's a spirit attached to one of the Indian artifacts, but it's not that. It's something else."

With our conversation flying back and forth we had almost forgot about Randy who was still in a trance.

"Paul, are you still here?"

"I never left."

"What do you want Anita and Chris to do?" Laurie asked Paul.

"It has to be buried. I didn't prepare myself." Paul sounded annoyed with himself.

"I think they're confused," Clare said.

"It should have been buried with me."

I told Laurie and Clare that Paul had not been buried but had been cremated and his ashes spread out over a mountaintop in Colorado.

"You mean you wanted it buried with your ashes instead of them being scattered out west?" Laurie asked.

"Yes, that's where they should have buried me."

"But that's not was stated in your will, Paul," I said exasperated. "We didn't know."

"Do you want Anita and Chris to bury it someplace now?" Clare asked.

"It should not fall into the wrong hands. It won't be good for them."

"If Anita and Chris find this object, where do you want them to bury it?"

"It should be put back where I got it."

Silence fell over the room.

"Ok. Where did you get it?" Laurie asked him.

"Peru."

That response from Paul completely took us by surprise and I couldn't help but laugh at the absurdity of the request.

"Well, it looks like we're going to Peru, Mom," Chris announced.

Laurie and Claire now laughed nervously too.

Again, silence.

Laurie broke in with her impression and a possible explanation of what Paul had just said.

"I think what I'm getting is that it was dug up from a grave site. A farmer on his land found it and he sold it to Paul. It was like, here's a rich American looking for artifacts and he's got the money to buy it, and he sold it to him. I don't think he really knew what he had in his possession. He had no idea what it was."

"Paul, do you know how difficult this would be for Anita and Chris?" Clare asked. "It would be impossible to put it back exactly where you bought it."

"I understand, I understand."

"Can't they just bury it under the ground?"

"No, they have to put it into a lead glass lined enclosure."

"So, it can't just be buried in the ground?" Laurie asked.

"No, it has to be inside a lead glass container. The artifact cannot get out past the lead in the glass."

"What the hell, man, can't we just put it in a lead lined container?" Chris asked.

"I don't think it's kryptonite, Chris," I said.

"How do you know?" Chris asked.

"Maybe a museum would want it and you can get rid of it that way," Clare suggested.

During the next few minutes we discussed the possibility of a museum being able to help us and accept the thing if we ever found it.

"Where are we going to find a lead glass container when we didn't even know how big this thing is or what it looks like," Chris asked. "This is crazy."

"Destroying the artifact...will not...help...the negativity."

"He's showing me a glass enclosure, but it's not glass, it's crystal," Laurie said.

"Yes, yes, yes."

"Do you guys have anything like that around here?" Laurie asked.

"No, but we have everything else," Chris answered sarcastically.

"Its power emits from the inside and cannot get out of the lead crystal. This is most imperative."

"Why did you have this in your house?" Laurie inquired.

"I was studying it...for a number of years."

"Is it harmful to anyone?" Clare asked.

"It didn't seem to hurt me."

"Oh, yeah? You're dead now," Chris mumbled under his breath.

"Shhh, Chris, cut it out," I whispered.

"Where did you keep it?" Clare asked.

"I moved it from room to room."

"In what room did you have it last?" Laurie asked.

"My bedroom."

"We took everything out of his bedroom and closet," I said.

"Can you tell me what color it is? Is it purple?" Laurie continued.

"No, many colors."

"Can you describe it to us as best you can?" Laurie asked more insistently.

"It has the ability to change shape...at will. It is not a good thing to have in the house." There was urgency in his voice.

"That doesn't sound like anything Native American to me," I said.

"It was not of this world," Paul insisted.

"What is it then...some kind of meteorite or something?" Chris asked.

"No, I think it's an *alien* artifact, guys," Laurie stated. She was dead serious.

"WHAT?" Chris asked. He looked at me and we had a "deer in the headlights" moment.

"This keeps getting better and better," I said sarcastically. "What the hell has he gotten my son and I involved in?" I could feel the hot blood rush to my face. I was furious.

"*I forgot to take care of this, I forgot,*" Paul was getting more upset. "*I'm sorry.*"

"It's not your fault, Paul," Clare said trying to comfort him.

"*Yes, it is.*"

Pause.

"*It's very, very valuable...very valuable. Don't let it get into the wrong hands.*"

"But now you've made Anita and Chris aware of it and we can now help you to move on," Clare said.

"*But I'm worried about these people.*"

"Right now we are more worried about you, Paul," Laurie said.

"*These are friends of mine...help them.*" He sounded as if he were frightened for us.

"You can better help them if you move on and cross over into the light," Clare said. "You can have your parents be your guides to help you cross over."

"*Yes, they came back to see me. Do you believe me?*"

Then, we heard an unknown voice on Chris' recorder. "*I want you to LEAVE this house.*"

"Yes, when you cross over you can come back to check on Anita and Chris and see if they found it."

"*I cannot move on until the problem is corrected.*"

Laurie knew this was a tough minded and determined spirit, but she kept trying to reason with him. "Paul, if you don't move into the light you will never be able to help Anita and Chris."

"The severity of the situation is very grave. I can't move on."

"Paul, you have to understand. We sold the house," I said. "You can't stay here. Please listen to them." I was now near tears pleading with him.

"If you go into the light you will meet with truth and purity and not be deceived," Clare said. "You won't meet any liars. You can help Anita and Chris by helping yourself."

"I've seen the deceivers."

"You can come back to visit Anita and Chris," Laurie reasoned with Paul.

"Yes."

"Do you want to move on now, Paul?"

"Go on...get." An unknown voice—not Paul's—was captured on Chris' recorder.

There was a brief silence.

"Do you want me to move on, Anita?"

"Yes, of course I do. I'm sad and I'm going to miss you, but you should be in the light, Paul. You were a good person, and you deserve to be there. You can't stay here. You have to move on. We'll be ok." I was crying hard now and hot tears were streaming down my cheeks.

"Then, so be it."

"Would you like us to call down the light for you, Paul? Do you see it?"

"The light is here."

"Good," Clare said. "We call upon the guides in the form of Hans, Paul's father and Hilda, Paul's mother, to join you in the light. I call upon the Archangels of Michael, Gabriel, Raphael, and Uriel and the Blue Angels to come down to help guide you to the light."

"I want to thank you for talking with us, Paul," Laurie said.

"Yes... you're welcome."

"Now you can move on."

"Then peace be with you."

"Peace be with you too," we all said in unison.

"Bye, Paul. We love you," I could barely choke out the words.

"Thank you for all you've done. I will be back to check on you and Chris."

"Ok." I was still crying, as this was an emotional moment for me.

"You must not grieve for me."

The room was silent for several seconds and then Randy came out of his trance. "He's gone," he said.

Moments later, everyone began to talk excitedly at once.

"That was pretty incredible,' Chris said.

"Intense," Clare said.

"Laurie, what in the world or should I say 'out of this world' was he talking about?" I had held back the question to both Clare and Laurie so as not to break their concentration in crossing Paul over.

"I don't know what this is. I've never experienced anything like it before and it has taken me by surprise," Laurie answered.

"You're surprised?" Chris exclaimed. He walked back over to Laurie to look at what she had drawn. He brought the paper over to me to get a better look at it near the table lamp and said, "Looks like a figure eight."

Randy seemed to be awake and aware of things that happened even though he was in a trance for half an hour. He now joined the living and our conversation.

"I don't know how you're supposed to find this object if it keeps changing its shape," Randy said. "But it definitely should be in a glass enclosure."

"Is he crossed over?" I asked Laurie. "Is he at peace?"

"We did cross Paul over, but there's something else. I'm afraid it's not over yet."

"What do you mean?" I asked.

"I just saw something that scared the hell out of me."

"What did you see, Laurie?" Chris asked.

"From where I'm sitting I have a clear view of the dining room and I just saw a two foot high creature scurrying along the carpet. It was scary as hell."

"Maybe it's the alien looking for his artifact," Chris remarked and handed the paper back to her. "I like aliens, like E.T.'s, but not that much."

"There was a vortex here that was opened and now it's pretty much closed," Laurie announced.

"Where was it?" I asked her.

"Down in the basement to the right of the back wall where that old wardrobe closet is."

"That's right under Paul's bedroom!" I exclaimed. "We always had a lot of poltergeist activity in that part of the basement."

"I was afraid of that. It could also have made Paul sick. Whatever this object was, it was here for a long time and created a portal. I think that's why you have so much activity in this house. There have been all kinds of spirits, not just him and his family, coming in and out of here and also other inter-dimensional beings."

"What are those?" Chris asked.

"Something like what I just saw in the dining room. They're not human."

"Can you get rid of them, Laurie?" I asked.

"Actually, I brought holy water with me; it's in my bag, but as I entered this house something laughed at me and said, *'That won't help.'*"

"I know. I have holy water in my bag too," Clare said. "It won't affect them. They have no Christian beliefs because they are older than Christianity and don't believe in the concept of holy water."

"Ok, so we're officially in hell!" Chris exclaimed, trying to make a joke.

"In a way, Chris, your friend was in hell; Paul was unaware of how powerful this thing was," Randy said. "But unfortunately he knows now. He couldn't move on until he was able to warn you about it. You're going to have to try and find that *thing.*"

"That's just great," I said loudly. "What else do I need to know?"

"Didn't you tell me that you've had some strange things happen in your house?" Laurie asked.

241

"I've had some really crazy dreams," Chris interjected.

"Like what?" Randy asked.

"Like people speaking German to me, trying to communicate. I understand German in my dreams, but when I wake up, I can't remember what they said. I'm going to start writing it all down. It's just been weird sleeping lately."

"Laurie, we haven't had anything happen in our house for several months. It's been very quiet," I said.

"Anita, you said that you cleared all his boxes and collectibles from his bedroom. Where are they now?" Laurie asked.

"They're in my house. Some stored in the basement. Why?"

"I don't think I like where this is going," Chris said.

"The portal is rapidly dissipating here. It's almost gone because everything is being stripped from this house. I think there's a good chance that with everything brought from this house, a paranormal vortex along with all its entities has been transferred to *your* house now!"

EPILOGUE

October 30, 2009

Hooray! Today we made settlement on the house. The lawyer had nothing but praise for me, explaining to the contractors what a superhuman feat I'd accomplished in just nine and a half months. During the signing of the final papers, he jokingly admitted that I'd done ninety-nine percent of the work while he pushed papers to earn his fee. We had removed over two tons of trash and recyclables, sent over seven-hundred bags to charities, packed over a hundred boxes for Paul's family, donated over eighty boxes of books to the library, plus removed and stored the dozens of collectables Paul had left me.

The estate wasn't closed yet, since only the house portion had been settled so far. The proceeds from the sale of the house were designated for an animal charity, so that major hurdle directed in the will was finished. The lawyer, in a previous meeting, assured me that we did not have to mention any of the paranormal activity to the new buyers, the contractors who are going to gut the house, remodel and resell it. Since it was never known to be a "haunted house" in any previous Pennsylvania real estate history (we only have our personal experiences), we didn't have to disclose it.

"Just let it be," said our lawyer. "I know these contractors, everything will be fine."

It could be another eight months before we could distribute to the other beneficiaries in Paul's will. To me, after what I'd been through, the rest would be a piece of cake.

I celebrated with my son and family that evening and we made a toast to a job well done. We couldn't believe the luxury of not having to worry about going to the house the next day. We were also happy that we avoided Halloween at the house and for good reason.

The last two weeks after we crossed Paul over, we still had some poltergeist activity, although we knew Paul wasn't among the residual spirits. Among the strangest occurrences was seeing that the pink hankie had moved from where it had been stuck in the ceiling rafters for four months to where it was now sitting, on top of the very wardrobe that Laurie mentioned was a portal. We had no idea how it got there or how the picture of a cemetery in Germany that showed the grave of one of Paul's ancestors, had suddenly appeared on the basement floor.

In spite of these recent events, Chris felt a positive change in the house and I felt confident the new owners wouldn't have any problems.

"We'll have to see the place when the contractors are finished," I said to Chris. "I'd be curious to see the changes to the basement."

As we were leaving the basement for the last time, we looked over at the grotesque grinning Leprechaun mask still sitting on a shelf. I didn't know why it was never thrown out.

"You want to take that with us, Mom?" Chris asked.

I just smiled at him. He always had a way to make me laugh, even when things were the most chaotic. "Are you kidding?"

Thanksgiving Day
November 26, 2009

We had a wonderful visit with my relatives and feasted on some delicious food. I kept my cousins spellbound as I related tales about the crazy incidents that had occurred at Paul's house during the past year.

They couldn't believe all the stories about the ghosts and kept telling me "You have to write a book, Anita!"

All has been quiet. Maybe Laurie was wrong, since we have no paranormal activity at my house at all. She said there were no guarantees or an exact science when dealing with the spirit realm.

We were trying to get back to living a more normal existence. Chris and I were trying to play "catch up" with our Christmas shopping, as I made plans for a wonderful get-together with Rose on Christmas Eve at my parents' house. This would be her first Christmas without her mother so it had to be special.

Christmas Eve
December 24, 2009

"Good morning, Mom. Can you believe it's Christmas Eve?"

"I know. You want some waffles and bacon?"

"That sounds good. What time are we going over to Nana and Poppy's?"

"I told Rose to be at your grandparents by five and..."

PING!

"Did you hear that?"

"Hear what?" In back of my mind the alarm bells were starting to go off but I quickly pushed aside any notions of anything unusual happening. "Come on Chris; put the maple syrup on the table."

"I don't know. I think I'm hearing things."

"So, I still have to pick up the crab cakes and some cans of minced clams for the pasta. We should be over there no later than..."

BANG!

ABOUT THE AUTHOR

Classically trained as a fine artist, Anita Jo Intenzo graduated with honors from Moore College of Art and Design in Philadelphia, earning a B.S. Degree in Art Education. She taught art classes at day and evening schools for 25 years. Her paintings currently hang in collections throughout the United States, and she has had several gallery shows.

She started restoring old photos over 35 years ago and created her business, Past Images by Anita, in 2000 where she preserves and restores family treasures: photos, paintings and antique dolls, so that their history will endure for future generations. Genealogical and historical societies seek her out for her expert consultations, lectures and appraisals.

In January of 2009, her life took a dramatic turn when, as executrix of a dear friend's estate, she became involved with the paranormal. As executrix, she was responsible for clearing his house and selling it. It did not take long after she began that task that Anita experienced real and often-frightening poltergeist activity there and soon began confronting true evil. She wrote this book as she was moved and profoundly changed by the experiences. She is now working on its terrifying sequel, DARK TRANSFERENCE.

Anita lives with her family and several resident ghosts, in the Philadelphia suburbs, on a property dating back to the 1800's.

Anita's website can be found at www.pastimagesbyanita.com

Printed in Great Britain
by Amazon.co.uk, Ltd.,
Marston Gate.